NORTHERN IRELAND ECONOMY: PERFORMANCE, PROSPECTS, POLICY

Northern Ireland Economy: Performance, Prospects, Policy

ESMOND BIRNIE
Department of Economics
The Queen's University of Belfast

DAVID M.W.N. HITCHENS
Professor of Applied Economics
Department of Economics
The Queen's University of Belfast

Routledge
Taylor & Francis Group
LONDON AND NEW YORK

First published 1999 by Ashgate Publishing

Reissued 2018 by Routledge
2 Park Square, Milton Park, Abingdon, Oxon, OX14 4RN
711 Third Avenue, New York, NY 10017, USA

Routledge is an imprint of the Taylor & Francis Group, an informa business

A Library of Congress record exists under LC control number: 98074436

ISBN 13: 978-1-138-33857-9 (hbk)
ISBN 13: 978-1-138-33858-6 (pbk)
ISBN 13: 978-0-429-44164-6 (ebk)

Contents

List of Figures

List of Tables

Foreword

This book aims to review the past development of, and future prospects for, the Northern Ireland economy. This is being done at a critical juncture given the potential economic impact of greater political stability and a devolved administration. Moreover various official reviews of economic policy were in progress during 1998. It is worth stressing that the final chapter (Chapter 8) (which attempts to draw together some of the conclusions on the likely future development of the economy and related policy responses) was written after the May 1998 Referendum result in favour of the Belfast Agreement.

This book updates the data and discussion contained in an earlier study by the authors (Hitchens, Wagner and Birnie (1990), *Closing the Productivity Gap*, Avebury). It does, however, differ from that work in its consideration of a wider range of economic sectors (Chapter 2 and 3) as well as of the impact of EU policies and developments on the regional economy (Chapter 5 and 6). The emphasis is empirical and applied but we seek to employ current theory on issues such economic growth and the advantages of clustered economic development.

Northern Ireland has had a longstanding position as a region which has lagged the average UK and EU economic performance in terms of a range of indicators (notably unemployment and living standards, Chapter 1). A critical question is therefore the extent to which a process of convergence with the more successful regions is occurring. Our investigation of manufacturing (Chapter 2), agriculture, business services and tourism (the main tradables goods and services sectors which have the greatest potential to become engines of growth, Chapter 3) between the inter-war period and the mid-1990s suggests that any underlying convergence towards Great Britain standards of performance (usually measured in terms of comparative labour productivity) has been weak.

By implication the problems hindering the increase in regional competitiveness are very deep seated (Chapter 4). We conclude that permanent peace might be a necessary condition for accelerated convergence towards the rest of the UK and EU (e.g. because it would enable greater in-flows of high quality physical and human capital) but it is not sufficient by itself (Chapter 8). The current extent and likely development of Northern Ireland-Republic of Ireland economic links is evaluated (Chapter 7).

The book is aimed at a number of markets. It is pitched at a sufficient level to be relevant to academics (university libraries), degree courses on the Northern Ireland economy and/or regional economics and policy makers. Much of it could be of use to A-level geography and economics students in Northern Ireland. At the same time we have aimed to make it accessible to the general reader.

During the final write-up of this book one of the authors (JEB) was elected to the New Northern Ireland Assembly. This could imply that he is about to discover that it is one thing to write about the formation of public policy and quite another thing to actually have to implement it!

The analysis of Northern Ireland-Great Britain manufacturing productivity differences during the 1980-92 using disaggregated Annual Census of Production data was funded by a grant from the Department of Economic Development in Belfast. We are very grateful to Dermot MacCann of the DED for this assistance. These comparisons would have been impossible but for the use of the computerised system of estimating the value of 'missing data', Professor Richard Harris (Portsmouth University) kindly allowed us to employ the procedure which he has developed. Mary Trainor ably directed this part of the research and arduous task of inputing the data was performed by Catherine Costello.

Professor Paul Teague (Visiting Professor at Cornell University, and University of Ulster) kindly read over a draft of the book. The data used in Figure 3.1 relating to tourist numbers was kindly granted by Dr Paul Gorecki, Director of the Northern Ireland Economic Council.

The final production of the manuscript was made possible with painstaking assistance from Mary Trainor (who also produced the diagrams) and in matters of typesetting and layout we were helped by the advice of the editorial staff of Ashgate.

The usual disclaimer applies.

J.E.B.
D.M.W.N.H.
August 1998

1 Living Standards and Unemployment

Summary

This Chapter provides a summary of the performance of the Northern Ireland economy. A comparative approach is employed in this Chapter and, indeed, throughout the rest of this book. Thus, the rest of the UK, the Republic of Ireland and other parts of the European Union are employed as standards of comparison. A brief historical outline of the development of the Irish economies since 1800 is presented in order to suggest implications for performance, prospects and policies in the 1990s. The Chapter concentrates on two indicators of macroeconomic performance: Gross Domestic Product (GDP) per capita (as a measure of living standards) and unemployment rates (as an indicator of the extent of full employment of resources in the labour market).

We argue that both these indicators are themselves influenced by the level of comparative labour productivity (output per person in work). GDP per employee, together with the size of the employed labour force as a proportion of the total population, is an immediate explanation of the level of GDP per head of the population. Labour productivity, along with relative wage and other labour costs, is a major influence on cost competitiveness, i.e. as labour productivity goes up, other things being equal, cost competitiveness would improve and hence the level of output and employment are also likely to increase. Given such relationships we present some summary data relating to Northern Ireland's comparative labour productivity performance in this Chapter. Chapters 2 and 3 will provide a more detailed consideration of this aspect of performance with special reference to the major tradable goods and services sectors.

Regional Economic Performance Considered Through a Comparative Method

When measuring the performance of an economy two indicators tend to be given special attention by economists. First, the level of income per head of the population and, second, the rate of unemployment. Income per head (often measured as GDP per head of the population though, as we shall argue below, Gross National Product (GNP) may sometimes be a more appropriate measure) is of significance because it determines the amount of economic resources available for both individual consumption and public spending. Unemployment matters as an indicator of the waste of potential human resources in the economy as well as the social distress suffered by those who are out of work.

Figures on the past and present performance of Northern Ireland with respect to both GDP per head and unemployment rates will now be presented. It is worth stressing at the beginning that most of the data presented in this book will be of a comparative nature, i.e. Northern Ireland will be compared to other parts of the world. Mostly these comparisons will be to either the rest of the UK (i.e. Great Britain) or the Republic of Ireland though, on occasions, some of the other members of the European Union (EU) will be used as well as the USA.[1]

Comparison to either the average for the UK or Great Britain is worthwhile given that the UK is the national economic and monetary union of which Northern Ireland is part. UK economic policies form the context within which any economic policies particular to Northern Ireland must operate. In fact, one of the aims of economic development strategies in Northern Ireland since the Second World War has been to close the gap in prosperity relative to the rest of the country (Harris, 1991). Great Britain also represents the largest 'external' market for most Northern Ireland businesses (see Table 6.1).

Comparisons with the Republic of Ireland are also of interest. This is because the two Irish economies were under common administration until the independence of southern Ireland from the UK in 1921 and since then (and especially since the Second World War) they have suffered similar problems and as a result have often introduced comparable policy responses (Kennedy, Giblin and McHugh, 1988; DFP, 1993; Bradley, 1996). At the same time, the Republic of Ireland offers a contrasting experience given that, first of all, it has the advantages and, indeed, sometimes disadvantages of being an independent nation state with much greater autonomy to set economic policy and, second, the human and material costs of the 'Troubles' since 1969 have largely been concentrated in Northern Ireland.

Historical Overview of Two Centuries of Development of the Two Irish Economies

One reason why it worthwhile comparing and contrasting the two Irish economies is because of interesting similarities and contrasts in terms of their economic development since the start of the nineteenth century. An overview of the past is also of value because it can shed light on the origins of some of the current competitiveness problems facing various sectors of the Northern Ireland economy. Chapter 2 will demonstrate that the shortfall in productivity performance in sectors such as manufacturing and agriculture has been present since the inter-war period and in this section we will show that there have been weaknesses in the economic performance of Northern Ireland throughout the period since 1800.

Pre-partition, 1800-1921

A notable similarity was the common administration during the period 1801-1921. A legacy of this has been broadly comparable institutions: the educational and training systems, trade unions, banks, types of business organisation and the civil service, for example. A very notable difference lay in the impact of the first industrial revolution (1780-1830s). The contrast was between the North which industrialised and the South which did so to a much lesser extent.

By 1914 there was a concentration of heavy industry around Belfast (shipbuilding and textiles) which was unique in the island. This area contained a large share of world output of certain commodities (8 per cent of all ships). The largest textile machinery, rope making and cigarette factories in the world were then operating within Belfast. This represented an example of the type of clustered economic development, i.e. firms linked together in networks through supply linkages, which some modern economists such as Porter (1990) have stressed as a key component of regional/national competitiveness.

There had been some industrialisation in the Dublin area too, e.g. in food processing, but this had not led on to growth in engineering. In what was to become the Republic of Ireland taken as a whole there was probably deindustrialisation in the early nineteenth century. Large numbers of jobs were shed in, for example, the pre-modern textiles industry.

Why was there this North-South difference? This problem has produced a prolonged debate, mainly amongst Southern Irish historians and economic historians as to 'why the (southern) Irish economy failed to industrialise in the nineteenth century?'. Sometimes this question is turned around to ask 'what advantage did the North have?'. Responses to this second question have included the following:

- Security in the system of land tenure which encouraged northern farmers to take a longer term view;
- The Protestant 'work ethic' (as in Max Weber (1930)) which promoted savings and investment and a modern commercial morality;
- Immigrant entrepreneurs coming from England, Scotland or Continental Europe: the Hugenots, Ritchie, Jaffa, Harland and Wolff, and Dunlop;
- 'Chance' happenings, i.e. small or chaotic variations which through cumulative processes, e.g. economies of scale or external economies, can eventually have very large effects.

According to the latter view it might take only fairly small differences between the extent of industrial development between Belfast and Dublin in the 1800s-1850s to ensure that the North would grow a cluster of manufacturing firms whereas the South did not.

The first two of these hypotheses had their adherents even in the mid-nineteenth century but the latter two find more favour with some modern economic historians (Ó'Gráda, 1994).

It is important to qualify this consideration of the contrasts between the two Irish economies. Even in 1914 Belfast was not that strong economically and some of the more recent problems stem from that period (see Chapters 2 and 3). It did not go through the 'second industrial revolution' (i.e. electrical engineering and chemicals from the 1880s onwards) and would in turn miss out on most of the third one which began in the post-Great Depression 1930s recovery, e.g. the development of cars and consumer goods manufacturing.

In fact, and notwithstanding the North's greater success in terms of industrialisation, levels of GDP per capita were similar in the two Irish economies in the years immediately before the First World War at about 50-60 per cent of the UK average. Crafts (1984) estimated GNP per capita in 1910 in Ireland as a whole at about three-quarters of Denmark, Switzerland, Germany and the Netherlands (i.e. the Continental leaders) and still considerably higher than Italy and Spain. (By the late 1990s GDP per capita in purchasing power parity terms, i.e. making allowance for differences in cost of living, in Spain was about equal to Northern Ireland and Italy's level was about one-fifth higher. In terms of GNP per capita the Republic of Ireland and Spain were at similar levels whilst Italy was substantially ahead of both.)

Partition, Great Depression and War, 1921 to early 1950s

Economic factors did have some part in causing the partition of Ireland between the 26 southern Counties and the six northern Counties in 1921. Unionists opposed Home Rule during 1886-1914 as a threat to Northern Ireland's access to markets within the British Empire. Nationalists, and later Sinn Fein, argued for Home Rule or complete independence in order to introduce trade protection. Ironically, both these political economies were to be somewhat disappointed by the way things actually turned out during the 1921 to early 1950s period.

As the initial post-First World War boom came to end Northern Ireland's grave structural disadvantages were revealed. The economy in general and manufacturing in particular was heavily concentrated on a few sectors; farming, linen and other textiles and shipbuilding. During the 1920s and early 1930s export demand for these products shrank whilst at the same time Northern Ireland was facing a situation where global supply capacity in these activities had expanded during the War. In fact, remaining within the UK had not guaranteed prosperity but Northern Ireland would probably have been even worse off if it had been administered from Dublin given the loss of access to UK markets and also UK unemployment benefit levels (Wilson, 1955; Gibson, 1996).

For its part, the Republic of Ireland during the 1930s-50s experienced the mixed blessing of protectionism. Employment in industry did increase but output growth decelerated in the 1950s (as the gains to import substitution were exhausted) and comparative productivity remained low

(Birnie, 1996). The impact of the 1939-45 War exacerbated whatever self-inflicted wounds had been created by national economic policy. The attempt to attain economic self-sufficiency was increased and by 1942 industrial output had fallen by one-quarter and in 1945 unemployment was still, officially, about 14 per cent. However, national income is reckoned to have risen by 7 per cent during 1938-45 and as a neutral the Republic of Ireland was better off than those Continental countries which had been fought over and devastated.

By the early 1950s the balance of economic fortunes did seem to be tipping decisively towards Northern Ireland. Why was this? At that time the Republic of Ireland seemed to be trapped within a vicious circle whereby slow growth within the protected home market was leading to out-migration and hence reduced aggregate demand whilst there was little encouragement to increase company competitiveness and export sales (Lee, 1989; Kennedy, 1990). During the 1950s industrial output grew at only 1.3 per cent annually. Comparative living standards actually dropped (to less than half of the UK average). In the 1950s there was a net emigration of 400,000.

Northern Ireland, in contrast, at least in economic terms, and notwithstanding the human and physical cost of such incidents as the 1941 Belfast air raids had a 'good war'. Rearmament and the consequent boost to government spending had provided something of a textbook Keynesian aggregate demand boost to the UK economy from the late 1930s onwards. From 1940 onwards this was felt very dramatically in Northern Ireland, even though Northern Ireland was characterised to an even greater extent than Great Britain (Barnett, 1986) by very poor industrial relations, work-force flexibility, labour productivity growth, levels of product and process innovation and standards of management in the key strategic industries such as aircraft, shipbuilding and textiles (Barton, 1995; Black, 1997). GDP per capita grew to about 70 per cent of the UK average (according to Isles and Cuthbert (1957) from 55 per cent in 1938 to 67 per cent in 1945). Thus, there was a widening advantage for Northern Ireland relative to the Republic of Ireland.

Benefiting from the 'Golden Age', 1958 to early 1970s

The beginning of this phase of Irish economic development can be identified by a sharp increase in the degree of Republic of Ireland's economic 'openness'. Tariffs came down and there was an end to restrictions on non-Irish ownership of firms operating within the Republic of Ireland. In parallel to these changes there was much increased encouragement given to inward investment (through the IDA agency). The profit tax incentive was introduced (initially in terms of 100 per cent tax relief on export earnings which was subsequently changed to a 10 per cent rate of corporate profit taxation for any manufacturing firm and selected service sectors).

Northern Ireland started off in the late 1950s from a position closer to free trade with the rest of the world. It also began to actively seek inward investment (e.g. man-made fibres such that by 1973 Northern Ireland was producing one-third of UK output in this sector). In both Irish economies GDP per head outgrew the UK average. At the end of period Northern Ireland GDP per capita had reached about three-quarters of the UK average and the Republic of Ireland about two-thirds. Manufacturing output in the Republic of Ireland grew by 5.9 per cent annually during 1959-72 and in Northern Ireland by 5.7 per cent per annum in the 1960s. Both Irish economies were enjoying the benefits of world conditions; the long post-war boom or 'full employment' era (Maddison, 1991).

Return to Difficult Times, 1973 to late 1980s

There was similarity between both economies in that both were hurt by the ending of the post-war international boom (the 1973 OPEC oil rise), though the Republic of Ireland was able to delay the consequences for a while through Keynesian policies but these were unsustainable in the longer term. Northern Ireland was quickly and badly hit by the consequences of the oil shock because energy and raw material costs in man-made fibres production rose and the global market for super oil tankers collapsed. Less inward investment of certain types was available and there was more competition for such investment as an increasing number of regions entered the market to attract mobile capital projects.

A major difference was, however, that the adverse economic impact of the Troubles was largely concentrated on Northern Ireland (the estimated impact by early 1980s was 25,000 to 40,000 jobs foregone) through unfavourable impacts on foreign direct investment, local investment, tourism, decision making and reduced labour mobility (see Chapters 4 and 8).

In both economies there were accumulating doubts as to traditional industrial policy. Inward investment proved costly to attract. The perception has been that there was insufficient emphasis on small and/or local firms It was felt that there was a need for more firms which were genuinely 'high tech' as opposed to multinationals which were often characterised as screwdriver or production platform branch plants with little or nothing by way of Research and Development (R&D) activities. The subsidisation of capital was judged to be characterised by a high degree of deadweight, i.e. investment which would have happened anyway, or displacement, i.e. subsidised firms grew at the expense of those which did not receive grants (see Chapters 7 and 8).

Late 1980s to date

In both Irish economies new industrial policies were introduced at the start of the 1990s (see Chapter 8). During the 1990s both Irish economies were apparently converging towards UK GDP per capita levels. Table 1.1 illustrates GDP growth performance in Northern Ireland relative to the UK average since 1971.

Table 1.1 Average annual GDP growth, Northern Ireland and the United Kingdom, 1971 onwards

	1971-80	1980-90	1990-95	1995-2000 forecast
Northern Ireland	1.8	2.7	2.1	2.2
United Kingdom	1.6	2.7	1.0	2.5

Source: Cambridge Econometrics (1997).

Table 1.2 illustrates recent economic growth rates in Northern Ireland compared to both the UK average and the Republic of Ireland (output growth rates for the manufacturing sector are also shown).

Table 1.2 Percentage annual real output growth, United Kingdom, Northern Ireland and the Republic of Ireland, 1985 to 1995

	Total Economy			Manufacturing Sector		
	UK	NI	ROI	UK	NI	ROI
1985	4.0	4.2	2.8	2.8	2.0	3.9
1986	4.0	8.2	0.1	1.3	3.0	2.0
1987	4.6	2.5	4.4	4.7	-1.2	10.3
1988	4.9	4.7	3.8	7.0	10.2	11.6
1989	2.3	2.6	6.4	4.5	6.8	12.0
1990	0.6	2.2	8.6	-0.2	13.9	4.5
1991	-2.1	2.7	1.6	-5.4	3.0	4.2
1992	-0.5	-0.2	3.2	-0.6	-5.1	10.1
1993	2.3	2.9	3.6	1.4	3.5	4.1
1994	4.0	5.1	6.7	4.2	10.9	12.1
1995	2.5	-	9.8	-	-	17.5

Source: Bradley and McCartan (1998).

As to prospects for the Northern Ireland economy some of the key questions include, e.g. can the ROI 'Celtic tiger'-boom continue? Can Northern Ireland continue to outperform the UK average? What would be the impact of 'permanent peace'? These issues are considered in Chapters 7 and 8.

The Comparative Record in Terms of Unemployment

Unemployment in Northern Ireland has traditionally been higher than in most European regions. Table 1.3 shows unemployment data for each member country as well as the regions with the lowest and highest unemployment rates.

Table 1.3 Unemployment and GDP per capita, Northern Ireland and the Republic of Ireland compared to the rest of the EU, 1994-5

	Standardised unemployment rate (%) 1995[a]	Long-term unemployment as % of total unemployment 1995[a]	GDP per capita, PPPs, EU15=100[b] 1994
EU 15	**10.7**	-	**100**
Belgium	**9.4**	**61.8**	**114**
Belgium lowest	6.9	46.7	91
Belgium highest	13.3	81.5	183
Denmark[c]	**7.1**	**28.2**	**114**
Finland	**18.1**	**29.9**	**91**
Finland lowest	6.2	-	91
Finland highest	18.2	30.0	126
France	**11.2**	**42.6**	**108**
France lowest	8.7	40.5	87
France highest	15.3	53.7	161
Germany[d]	**8.2**	**47.8**	**110**
Germany lowest	4.9	39.6	196
Germany highest	16.7	56.2	57
Greece	**9.1**	**50.9**	**65**
Greece lowest	4.5	50.7	57
Greece highest	11.0	50.2	73
Republic of Ireland[c]	**14.3**	**51.1**	**88**
Italy	**12.0**	**61.5**	**102**
Italy lowest	6.0	43.8	131
Italy highest	25.9	72.8	68
Luxembourg[c]	**2.7**	**24.0**	**169**
Netherlands	**7.3**	**44.4**	**105**
Netherlands lowest	6.9	46.4	101
Netherlands highest	8.9	47.4	102
Portugal	**7.1**	**48.7**	**67**
Portugal lowest	4.6	67.2	48
Portugal highest	7.8	60.0	68
Spain	**22.7**	**54.4**	**76**
Spain lowest	7.8	60.0	58
Spain highest	18.5	63.0	64

Table 1.3 ctd...

	Standardised unemployment rate (%) 1995[a]	Long-term unemployment as % of total unemployment 1995[a]	GDP per capita, PPPs, EU15=100[b] 1994
Sweden[c]	**9.1**	-	**98**
United Kingdom	**8.8**	**43.1**	**99**
UK lowest	6.7	35.2	117
Northern Ireland (UK highest)	*13.0*	*51.6*	*80*

[a] Unemployment defined according to a standardised economic activity classification. Long-term unemployed being those out of work for more than one year. The regional long-term unemployment and GDP data correspond to whichever regions had the lowest or highest rates of *total* unemployment.
[b] GDP is a measure of the total value of goods and services produced during each year. Although GDP is often used in international comparisons, peculiarities of the Republic of Ireland economy imply that it is an inappropriate indicator of living standards (see below) which biases measured comparative productivity in an upwards direction. The purchasing power parity (PPPs) based calculations make allowance for variations in the cost of living.
[c] No sub-national regional breakdown was available.
[d] Including the former East Germany.

Source: Office for National Statistics (ONS) (1997a).

As is well known, the average unemployment rate in Northern Ireland has always exceeded the average for the rest of the UK, see Figure 1.1. Indeed, the Northern Ireland unemployment rate has traditionally been the highest of any major UK region (in recent years the UK statistical authorities have begun to publish unemployment data for the Merseyside region alongside the standard regions for which data was previously available; Merseyside has had higher unemployment rates than Northern Ireland). It is also of note that Northern Ireland has a higher proportion of long-term unemployed (i.e. those without a job for longer than one year) as well and in fact this problem is more marked in Northern Ireland than in almost any other EU region (see Tables 1.3 and 1.4).

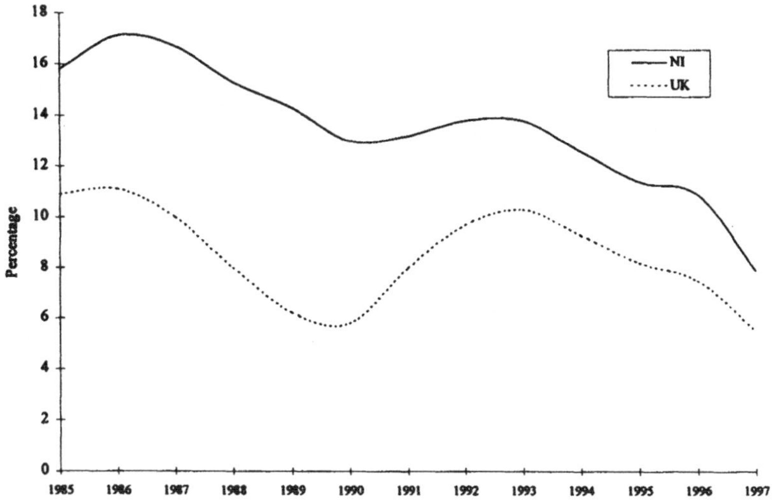

Figure 1.1 Percentage unemployment rate[a], Northern Ireland and the United Kingdom, June, 1985 to 1997[b]

[a] The number of unemployment-related benefit claimants as a percentage of the estimated total workforce i.e. claimants, employees in employment, self-employed, participants on work-related government-supported training programmes and HM Forces.
[b] July 1997.

Source: ONS (1997b, 1997c).

At the same time, as Table 1.4 shows, the rate of total unemployment, and especially short-term unemployment, in Northern Ireland has fallen rapidly in the 1990s towards the UK average. It is, however, unclear how far this represents a real improvement in labour market performance or simply changes in the rigour with which eligibility for unemployment benefit (e.g. with the introduction of the Job Seeker's Allowance) was being policed.[2]

Table 1.4 Short and long-term[a] unemployment rates[b], Northern Ireland and Great Britain, selected years, 1985 to 1996[c]

	NI short-term rate	NI long-term rate	NI > 5 years rate	GB short-term rate	GB long-term rate	GB > 5 years rate
1985	8.4	8.6	1.4	6.9	4.7	0.5
1987	8.5	8.9	2.4	6.2	4.5	0.9
1989	6.6	8.0	2.8	3.9	2.5	0.7
1991	6.4	6.5	2.6	5.7	1.8	0.4
1993	6.4	7.5	2.6	6.8	3.7	0.4
1994	5.7	7.1	2.4	6.0	3.6	0.4
1995	4.9	6.5	2.3	5.3	3.1	0.4
1996	5.1	6.0	2.3	5.1	2.8	0.5

[a] The rate for those unemployed for more than 5 years is included in the long-term rate (i.e. all those unemployed for more than 1 year).
[b] All rates are as a percentage of the total workforce.
[c] Figures relate to April of each year.

Source: Training and Employment Agency (T&EA) quoted in NIEC (1997c).

Table 1.5 Qualifications held by those in employment, short-term unemployment and long-term unemployment, Northern Ireland, Winter 1995-96 (% of total)

	Employed	Short-term unemployed*	Long-term unemployed*
Higher qualifications	23	9	4
GCE A-level or equivalent	30	31	29
GCE O-level or equivalent	17	18	11
Other qualifications	9	13	5
No qualifications	22	30	51
Total	100	100	100

* Using an International Labour Organisation (ILO) definition of unemployment (i.e. based on availability for work).

Source: As Table 1.4.

Long-term unemployment persists as a serious social and economic problem in Northern Ireland. As Table 1.5 shows, more than half of those out of work for more than one year have no formal qualifications. The long-term unemployed in Northern Ireland are not equally distributed geographically nor, indeed, according to religious denomination. They are concentrated in inner city Belfast and in Northern Ireland west of the river Bann. There are in fact substantial variations in long-term unemployment rates even between neighbouring Travel to Work Areas (TTWAs). For example, Ballymena had a long term unemployment rate of 3.8 per cent in April 1996, it also had the lowest total unemployment rate of any TTWA, but the contiguous TTWAs had long-term unemployment rates of 6.9 per cent, 7.4 per cent and 5.0 per cent. Such spatial differences, reflecting both problems of accessibility and perceived or real sectarian intimidation in various work places, have led Borooah, McKee, Heaton and Collins (1995) to comment that Northern Ireland

> ... should not be seen as an area over which workers and job seekers, regardless of religion, move freely but rather as a constellation of geographically segmented labour markets between which mobility is extremely limited.

This is consistent with a survey of the long-term unemployed in mainly Catholic West Belfast, which highlighted the perceived threat of intimidation as an important factor restricting job search (Sheehan and Tomlinson, 1996). Overall, the long-term unemployed are disproportionately male, aged thirty or more and Catholic (NIEC, 1997c).

Though unemployment levels remain a significant problem, the Northern Ireland economy has nevertheless had an impressive record in terms of job creation (Tables 1.6 and 1.7) and in fact outperformed the UK average in this respect since the 1980s. The immediate explanation of this paradox has been the relatively rapid growth of labour supply in Northern Ireland (see Note 2 at the end of this Chapter).

Table 1.6 Percentage annual employment growth, United Kingdom, Northern Ireland and the Republic of Ireland, 1985 to 1995

	Total Economy			Manufacturing Sector		
	UK	NI	ROI	UK	NI	ROI
1985	0.9	-2.2	-2.2	-0.9	0.7	-2.7
1986	-0.2	3.9	0.2	-2.4	-4.5	1.9
1987	0.9	0.2	0.8	-1.4	-1.3	-1.8
1988	3.1	3.2	0.0	0.8	2.0	0.0
1989	1.8	2.6	-0.2	-0.3	0.5	5.6
1990	1.1	2.7	4.2	-2.5	-0.1	2.6
1991	-2.9	0.6	0.0	-8.9	-1.0	-0.4
1992	-1.6	-0.3	0.8	-5.1	-2.5	0.0
1993	-1.5	-0.3	0.4	-4.4	-2.1	-1.3
1994	1.0	-0.1	3.0	0.7	2.0	4.4
1995	0.8	3.2	4.8	2.5	2.9	4.6

Source: Bradley and McCartan (1998).

Table 1.7 Employment in Northern Ireland sectors, 1987 to 1996

	Manufacturing employees in employment	Service employees in employment	Total employees in employment	Self-employed
1987	101,880	346,170	504,110	83,200
1988	103,950	356,610	517,210	-
1989	104,510	365,470	526,640	-
1990	104,370	376,330	538,160	-
1991	103,280	383,960	542,070	-
1992	100,720	390,080	543,570	-
1993	98,570	396,210	546,410	-
1994	100,590	400,790	557,930	-
1995	103,460	420,140	573,160	-
1996	101,790	423,190	572,610	77,700

Source: Northern Ireland Statistics and Research Agency (1997).

The Comparative Record in Terms of Income per Head

A number of recent studies have demonstrated a tendency within the developed world for regions/countries with relatively low levels of income per capita to grow more rapidly than those which start on higher levels of income per capita (Barro and Sala-i-Martin, 1991, 1995). This is the process of so-called catch-up or convergence.

The low income per capita region can enjoy a period of relatively rapid growth through copying the superior production and management techniques in the more advanced regions and also through upgrading its level of capital stock or indeed human capital (i.e. training and skills) per worker. This explanation of economic growth reflects the so-called neoclassical growth theory (Mankiw, Romer and Weill, 1992).

Table 1.8 indicates that levels of GDP per head in Northern Ireland have caught up and converged towards the UK average level at only a slow rate during the last seventy years. Indeed, as our review of the economic history of Northern Ireland implied, that process of convergence seems to have been discontinuous: fairly large gains during the Second World War, something of a relapse during the 1950s, resumption of convergence during the 1960s, a mixed record after the oil shocks and a gain of several percentage points as the rest of the UK (but not Northern Ireland (NIEC, 1993b)) suffered a decline in GDP levels during the 1990-92 recession. Given that the UK as a whole was falling behind in the international league tables during much of the post-War period the implication is that Northern Ireland has made only limited progress in catching up relative to the richest parts of the EU, represented in Table 1.8 by West Germany/Germany, or, indeed, relative to the USA.

The experience of the Republic of Ireland since the late 1980s appears to be somewhat different and markedly superior (FitzGerald, 1997; Walsh, 1997). There was a substantial lag behind both Northern Ireland and the UK average throughout the first 65 years of Independence (Ó'Gráda and O'Rourke, 1996). Since the late 1980s, however, levels of GDP per capita have reached those in Northern Ireland and have perhaps reached equality with the UK average as well during 1996 or 1997 (Michie and Sheehan, 1996).

Table 1.8 GDP per capita in Northern Ireland (NI) compared to the United Kingdom (UK), Republic of Ireland (ROI), Germany* and the USA, 1926 to 1995

	NI/UK (% of UK level) UK=100	ROI/UK (% of UK level) UK=100	NI/ Germany (% of German level) Germany = 100	NI/USA (% of USA level) USA = 100	ROI/ Germany (% of German level) Germany = 100	ROI/ USA (% of USA level) USA = 100
1926	62	51	86	38	71	31
1947	71	46	161	44	105	28
1960	63	47	69	43	52	32
1973	73	54	71	49	53	36
1986	80	60	69	55	53	43
1991	82	77	65	58	61	55
1994	82	86	67* *74*	57	70* *77*	60
1995	83	91	*69*	58	*82*	64

* The pre-1994 comparisons for Germany relate to the territory within the 1949-90 frontiers, i.e. West Germany. The 1994 and 1995 results in italics are based on comparisons to unified Germany including East Germany.

Source: Kennedy, Giblin and McHugh (1988); Hitchens, Wagner and Birnie (1990); Maddison (1991); SOEC (1996); ONS (1997a).

However, a lot of caution needs to be used in interpreting these results. As Chapter 7 of this book will argue, all the Republic of Ireland national income statistics are liable to exaggeration given the accounting practices of some of the foreign owned companies which operate there (so-called 'transfer pricing'). What is certain is that a considerable part of measured Republic of Ireland GDP is not actually available for consumption within that state. In 1995 roughly 13 per cent of GDP represented a net outflow of resources to, firstly, repatriate the profits made by American, European and Far Eastern companies and, secondly, to pay off interest on the considerable overseas debt which was accumulated during the 1970s.

In other words, an alternative measure, Gross National Product (GNP), is a more appropriate, though still not perfect, indicator of living standards in the Republic of Ireland (see Chapter 7 for a direct comparison of levels of consumer and public spending in the two Irish economies which indicates that Northern Ireland living standards were higher by 15 to 26 per cent in 1994). In 1995 GNP per head in the Republic was still about one-fifth lower than the UK average.

There is a very large literature on international differences in levels of GDP per capita and especially the UK economy's relative decline during 1950s-70s (Crafts, 1993) and also as to why the USA lead relative to the rest of the world narrowed after the Second World War (Baumol, Blackman and Wolff, 1989; Dertouzous, Lester and Solow, 1989). A common theme has been to stress the role of labour productivity, i.e. in the long-run for most countries the relative level of output per worker in the major economic sectors will be the primary determinant of their comparative level of national income per head.

Strictly speaking the immediate explanation of levels of comparative GDP per head of the population is GDP per head of the employed labour force multiplied by the labour force as a proportion of the total population. The UK, including Northern Ireland, has tended to lie above the European average in terms of the labour force as a proportion of the population. This implies that direct responsibility for the relatively low GDP per capita in the UK, including Northern Ireland, lies with relatively low GDP per person in employment. The Republic of Ireland has a contrasting record. During the last 10 to 15 years GDP per person in employment has almost completely converged to the EU average but GDP per head has remained less than the EU average because the Republic of Ireland still has one of the lowest proportions of the population in work of any European country.

The data shown in Table 1.9 implies that part of the explanation for the comparatively low level of GDP per capita in Northern Ireland is that the proportion of the population in work lies below the UK average.

Table 1.9 Percentage of the population in work, 1986 and 1993

	1986	1993
Northern Ireland	36	38
Republic of Ireland	30	32
United Kingdom	43	44
USA	45	46
Japan	48	52
Germany*	41	45
France	38	38
Canada	46	45

* West Germany in 1986; East Germany and West Germany in 1993.

Source: HM Treasury (1989); CSO (1990); Hitchens, Wagner and Birnie (1990); SOEC (1995); PPRU (1996).

Table 1.10 Northern Ireland relative productivity and cost competitiveness, percentage of the United Kingdom average level (NI/UK, UK = 100)

	GDP per person engaged as a % of the UK level		Unit labour cost as a % of the UK level	
	1989	1992	1989	1992
Agriculture	74	68	83	88
Utilities	89	86	123	114
Manufacturing	82	83	106	106
Construction	91	83	96	99
Distribution	91	93	90	87
Transport and communications	95	91	96	100
Financial	107	103	82	83
Other services	103	113	88	81
Total economy	89	87	103	103

Source: Northern Ireland Economic Research Centre (NIERC) quoted in DFP (1993).

Table 1.10 shows the relative level of labour productivity of broadly defined sectors of the Northern Ireland economy in 1989 and 1992. Since GDP levels per person in employment usually fall below the UK average this also provides part of the explanation for the relatively low GDP per capita level in Northern Ireland.

Table 1.10 also shows the development of relative unit costs in Northern Ireland relative to the UK (relative unit labour costs being the ratio of relative total labour costs, both wage and non-wage, and relative productivities). In Table 1.10 unit cost measures of greater than 100 would imply that it was costing Northern Ireland firms more in terms of labour input to produce one unit of output than was the case for their counterparts in the rest of the UK. These results suggest that in the early 1990s the Northern Ireland economy as a whole was less cost competitive than the UK economy on average though responsibility for these relatively high unit costs was concentrated in the utilities (i.e. mainly electricity generation) and manufacturing sectors.

The reason for this was that because productivity levels were so much lower than the UK average that, even though levels of wages and salaries were also relatively low, labour costs were not sufficiently low to compensate for the comparatively low productivity levels. The implication was that at least in the early 1990s unit costs, i.e. the cost per unit of output produced, in Northern Ireland exceeded the UK average. It is important to stress that to the extent that Northern Ireland industry was thus uncompetitive on cost this could have been a contributory factor to the relatively high level of unemployment (DTI, 1983; Dignan, 1994). Since 1992 the situation with respect to relative cost competitiveness may have 'improved' in the sense that relative wage levels in Northern Ireland have fallen (see Chapter 2). This, however, is not really a desirable route to fuller employment through greater competitiveness. The implication would be that Northern Ireland has obtained more employment but only at the cost of a lower level of living standards. The introduction of a national minimum wage will in any case constrain the ability of Northern Ireland to further reduce wages relative to Great Britain (NIEC, 1998a).

Notes

1. Sometimes Northern Ireland's performance has been compared to the UK average. Strictly speaking this procedure is not satisfactory given that it implies that Northern Ireland is being compared to a multi-regional average which is itself partly determined by that Northern Ireland performance. However, given that Northern Ireland's weight within total UK employment, GDP or manufactured output is usually no more than 2 per cent, any bias is likely to be negligible.
2. Part of the explanation of the persistently relatively high unemployment rates in Northern Ireland has been that the rate of natural increase of the population has tended to outstrip the growth in labour demand even though employment growth in Northern Ireland has been better than the EU and UK averages since 1989 (Gudgin, 1998).

   The Northern Ireland birth rate fell from about 25 per 1,000 of the population at its peak in 1965 to about 17 per 1,000 in 1975. In contrast, in England and Wales the decline was from 12 per 1,000 to 7 per 1,000. Table 1.11 shows that compared to the rest of the UK or the EU or, indeed, the Republic of Ireland, Northern Ireland in 1989-91 had an unusually high rate of natural increase.

Table 1.11 Natural population increase, average annual rates, Northern Ireland, England and Wales, Scotland, Republic of Ireland and European Union, 1989 to 1991, rates per 1000 population

	Natural increase	Birth rate	Death rate
Northern Ireland	6.9	16.6	9.7
England and Wales	2.4	13.6	11.2
Scotland	0.5	12.8	12.3
United Kingdom	2.4	13.7	11.3
Republic of Ireland	5.9	14.9	9.0
European Union	1.9	11.9	10.0

Source: Compton (1995).

Other things being equal, this relatively rapid rate of natural increase at the start of the 1990s will translate into a rapid growth in labour force demand at the end of the first decade of the twenty-first century. This begs the question whether the local economy will be able to generate jobs at a sufficient rate to keep pace with such a supply. However, it is unlikely that other things will be equal. Table 1.12 shows the growth in Northern Ireland's population between 1986 and 1995 and also the levels of net migration which are partly caused by the disequilibrium in the labour market between growth in labour supply and labour demand. The period 1991-94 was unusual in that net in-migration occurred; the Great Britain economy was then still to recover from the very severe 1990-92 recession whereas the Northern Ireland economy emerged from that recession largely unscathed (NIEC, 1993b).

Table 1.12 Northern Ireland population and net migration, 1986 to 1995 and projections 1999 to 2024

	Population	Net migration (+ outflow, - inflow)
1986	1,566,800	+3,600
1987	1,575,100	+5,900
1988	1,578,000	+7,900
1989	1,583,000	+6,400
1990	1,589,400	+4,600
1991	1,601,400	-2,000
1992	1,618,400	-3,650
1993	1,631,800	-3,600
1994	1,641,700	-1,064
1995	1,649,000	+239
1999	1,669,000	-
2009	1,696,000	-
2019	1,724,000	-
2024	1,741,000	-

Source: Northern Ireland Statistics and Research Agency (1997).

2 Sectoral Competitiveness: Manufacturing

Summary

The previous Chapter has demonstrated Northern Ireland's persistently unfavourable performance relative to the rest of the UK in terms of two indicators, unemployment and GDP per capita. Comparative labour productivity was identified as a critical variable. This is partly because with wages and other labour costs held constant an increase in relative labour productivity would increase comparative cost competitiveness. This in turn might be expected to boost sales, output and hence employment (with a consequent reduction in unemployment). Other things being equal, one would also expect an increase in labour productivity to have a direct and beneficial impact on GDP per capita. For these reasons we follow Porter (1990), DTI (1996), NIEC (1998b) and others in regarding relative labour productivity levels as one of the most useful summary indicators of regional/national competitiveness.

In this Chapter and Chapter 3 we evaluate the competitiveness performance of the main tradables sectors, manufacturing, agriculture, tourism and business services, by considering (as far as is possible) comparative productivity performance. We highlight the tradables activities because it is here that there is likely to be the greatest scope to attain net additions to Northern Ireland's total output and employment through either increasing extra-regional sales or through reducing imports into the region (Hitchens and Birnie, 1994). Manufacturing is considered in this Chapter. Manufactured products still make up the majority of world trade.[1]

Northern Ireland Manufacturing Performance Compared to International Productivity Levels

In addition to aggregate productivity comparisons for total manufacturing, Table 2.1 also illustrates the comparative performance of five individual manufacturing industries. Mechanical engineering & transport equipment and electrical & electronic engineering were chosen to illustrate the position with respect to 'higher technology activities' which have relatively high intensity of inputs of skilled labour, capital and R&D. In contrast, food processing, textiles and clothing are more indicative of so-called 'traditional' manufacturing which has less reliance on specialised or sophisticated inputs. It would be expected that the various countries in Table 2.1, which are drawn from the first world, third world and former communist bloc, would, given their varying histories of industrial development, display differing factor proportions (i.e. extent of mechanisation and automation) and hence contrasting comparative performance. Thus, apart from the UK, Table 2.1 includes the two global productivity leaders (the USA and Japan), a group of major north western European economies (West Germany, France and the Netherlands), two of the late industrialisers of southern Europe (Italy and Spain), three eastern European economies and, finally, three of the so-called Newly Industrialised Countries (Brazil, Mexico and South Korea), as well as the two Irish economies. The comparisons in this Table relate mostly to 1987. International comparisons of productivity *levels* as opposed to consideration of growth rates are rarely very up-to-date (van Ark, 1993). This is because production census data tends to become available only after a substantial time lag. Furthermore, detailed comparisons using relative output price levels are time consuming. It is likely that the relative positions established for 1987 persisted about a decade later (later in this Chapter we provide updated Northern Ireland/Great Britain comparisons into the early 1990s).

Table 2.1 Comparative manufacturing productivity, 1987, levels of value added per employee as a per cent of the UK level (UK = 100), (comparisons made using output prices of principal products; unit value ratios)

	Total manuf.	Food processing	Mech. eng. & transp. equip.	Electrical & electronic eng.	Textiles	Clothing
Northern Ireland	77	90	58	70	88	85
USA	187	207	161	182	120	158
Japan	160	56	224	192	101	106
West Germany	113	114	122	90	104	113
France	117	115[a]	131[a]	107[a]	93[a]	120[a]
Netherlands	143	141	95	140	174	123
Italy	111[b]	128[c]	-	-	138[c]	-
Spain[a]	88	95	77	77	93	93
Republic of Ireland	118 (158)	148 *meat*[d] 88 *dairy*[d] 84 *bread*[d] 40 *grain milling*[d]	114	(264)	100	73
East Germany	34	52	-	-	35	-
Czech Republic	20	18	20	-	21	23
Hungary	23	9	28	-	23	25
Brazil	82[e]	48	-	-	-	-
Mexico	74[e]	52	-	-	-	-
South Korea	49	27	71	74	41	32

[a] 1984.
[b] 1989.
[c] 1986
[d] 1985.
[e] 1975.

Source and Notes:
Northern Ireland: Annual Census of Production (1987) comparisons of gross value added (GVA) per head. GVA is defined as the total sales value of output, adjusted for changes in stocks of unsold goods, minus all the industrial inputs (such as raw materials and energy) and also the so-called non-industrial services (such as bought in business services like marketing, design and consultancy).
USA: van Ark (1992) comparisons of GVA.
Japan: van Ark (1993) Japan/USA comparison (net output) linked to van Ark (1992) for UK/USA. Net output differs from GVA in that the value of the non-industrial services is not subtracted.
West Germany: O'Mahony (1992) comparisons of GVA. Food processing is represented by food, drink and tobacco combined and mechanical engineering etc. by mechanical engineering alone.
France: van Ark (1993) comparisons of GVA. Food processing is represented by food and drink combined.
Netherlands: van Ark (1993) comparisons of GVA. Food processing is represented by food and drink combined.
Italy: Total manufacturing from Broadberry (1994). Sectoral results from SOEC (1990) for GVA in 1987 but using 1985 PPPs.
Spain: van Ark (1994a) comparisons of GVA. Mechanical engineering etc. and electrical engineering etc. combined, as are textiles and clothing.
Republic of Ireland: Birnie (1996) comparisons of net output for 1985 updated using indices of nominal net output change 1985-87, output price deflators and employment change. Results shown in parenthesis are likely to include a large component attributable to transfer pricing. The total manufacturing result for 1985 was re-estimated on the assumption that the scale of transfer pricing could be indicated by the volume of profit outflows (these were equivalent to 25.4 per cent of total net output). The assumption was that the aim of any transfer pricing would be to maximise post-tax profits and then some of these would be repatriated to the home country. NESC (1993a) attributed 90 per cent of total outflows to manufacturing and other industrial activities. Murphy (1994, 1996) argued that the official figures might under-estimate the true scale of outflows. Significantly, our estimate of ROI/UK productivity in 1985 in the absence of transfer pricing (110) is very close to the result implied by the 1968 comparative productivity measurement updated to 1985 using indices of output and employment (the relatively small scale of the externally owned sector at the earlier date makes it unlikely that there was

substantial transfer pricing at that stage; deflated gross output indices would probably be less subject to distortion through transfer pricing than measurements of net output).
East Germany: van Ark (1994b) comparison of East Germany/West Germany (GVA) for 1987 linked to UK/West Germany (van Ark, 1993).
Czech Republic: Hitchens, Birnie, Hamar, Wagner and Zemplinerova (1995) comparison of Czech Republic/West Germany for 1993 (GVA) linked to UK/West Germany for 1987 (van Ark, 1993). Clothing and textiles are combined in the Czech Republic/West Germany comparisons.
Hungary: Hitchens, Birnie, Hamar, Wagner and Zemplinerova (1995) comparison of Hungary/west Germany for 1993 (GVA) linked to UK/West Germany for 1987 (van Ark, 1993). Clothing and textiles are combined in the Hungary/West Germany comparisons.
Brazil: van Ark (1993) comparison of Brazil/USA for 1975 (GVA) linked to an implied UK/USA result for 1975 (van Ark, 1993). Food processing; Brazil/USA (McKinsey, 1993) for 1987 linked to UK/USA (van Ark, 1992).
Mexico: van Ark (1993) comparison of Mexico/USA for 1975 (GVA) linked to an implied UK/USA result for 1975 (van Ark, 1993). Food processing; Mexico/USA (McKinsey, 1993) for 1987 linked to UK/USA (van Ark, 1992).
South Korea: South Korea/USA comparison from van Ark (1993) (GVA) linked to UK/USA (van Ark, 1992).
These comparisons generally relate to those plants with 20 or more persons engaged.

When the results in Table 2.1 are set alongside those for earlier years from previous studies (Rostas, 1948; Paige and Bombach, 1958; Smith, Hitchens and Davies, 1982; Wagner and van Ark, 1996) then three stylised facts seem to emerge regarding the international pattern of productivity differentials:

- The USA remains the overall world productivity leader though it has been effectively challenged by Japan in several sectors, particularly in metals, cars and engineering;
- The continental western European economies sustained marked productivity convergence relative to the USA during the 1950s-70s though this convergence slowed or came to a halt in the period since the 1970s recessions;
- The UK was overtaken by most of the continental western European economies during the 1950s and 1960s. The so-called British 'productivity miracle' post-1979 represents a strong though still

incomplete convergence to the European productivity leaders (DTI, 1995, 1996).

Northern Ireland manufacturing, for its part, has been characterised by a substantial productivity shortfall (30 to 15 per cent) relative to the UK average throughout the period for which statistics are available (i.e. 1913-92) albeit with a weak trend of convergence during 1960-73. Republic of Ireland manufacturing productivity remained 20 per cent below the UK level throughout the 1930s-60s. By the early 1980s, however, a substantial productivity advantage had been established and this was increasing. Significantly, the high *average* productivity in manufacturing in the Republic of Ireland, was not reflected in indigenously owned firms. There are a number of indications that much of the productivity advantage in the foreign owned firms is attributable to transfer pricing, that is, the artificial manipulation by international companies of their balance sheets in order to maximise profits and hence measured value added in their Irish subsidiaries in order to extract the maximum advantage from a relatively low rate of corporate profit taxation (Birnie, 1996; Birnie and Hitchens, 1998).

How might these stylised facts be explained? The long established productivity advantage of the USA has been explained in terms of:

- Relative factor supplies: during the nineteenth century the shortage of labour in the USA economy relative to the abundance of natural resources encouraged American firms to pioneer mechanisation;
- Scale economies: USA firms, unlike their European counterparts, had the advantage of selling to a single very large home market. his implied, for example, that product types could be standardised and hence unit costs of production reduced through use of long production runs;
- R&D: American firms led the way in terms of the appliance of scientific research to industrial innovation, e.g. large corporations setting up their own R&D departments.

The post-Second World War partial convergence by Japan and Europe towards the USA could be explained in terms of the following:

- A catch up phenomenon; after 1945 there was a very large gap between American productivity levels and those in the rest of the western economies (Maddison, 1991). Thus other economies had the opportunity to make relatively easy gains to output per head and efficiency simply by copying USA practice;
- Capital per head now often equals the USA; in Japan and Germany levels of capital per worker no longer lag behind those in America (Wagner and van Ark, 1996);
- Much of human capital difference has been removed; various crude measures of educational qualifications (e.g. years of schooling) suggest that America had an advantage relative to western Europe and Japan at the start of the 1950s (Denison, 1967) but these regions now have caught up with or even surpassed the USA (Wagner and van Ark, 1996).

As to the UK's relative decline in terms of comparative manufacturing productivity during the pre-1979 period, human capital has received most attention, i.e. the impact of the output from the school and training system on the qualifications, experience and flexibility of the shop-floor labour force plus management (Prais, 1981; Barnett, 1986; Matthews, 1988). This explanation probably has some application to the particular case of Northern Ireland and also to the indigenously owned sector of manufacturing in the Republic of Ireland (Hitchens, Wagner and Birnie, 1990). A later section of this Chapter will consider how far human capital or, indeed, some of the other factors which have been identified in international productivity studies, apply to Northern Ireland.

Northern Ireland Comparative Manufacturing Productivity in Recent Years

Gross value added (GVA) is defined as the total sales value of output minus the cost of industrial inputs such as raw materials and energy and also non-industrial inputs such as certain bought in services (e.g. advertising, consultancy, rents and rates, postage, advertising, transport) and in principle is the best measure of 'value added'. It is, however, only available in more recent production census data (from 1973 onwards) and so 'net output' often has to be used. This differs from GVA by its inclusion of the non-industrial services.

Table 2.2 Northern Ireland comparative gross value added per head, total manufacturing, 1973 to 1992

	Gross value added per employee (NI/GB, GB = 100) based on SIC 1968	Gross value added per employee (NI/GB, GB = 100) based on SIC 1980
1973	94	-
1974	83	-
1975	93	-
1976	88	-
1977	81	-
1978	74	-
1979	79	-
1980	79	80
1981	88	86
1982	79	81
1983	81	84
1984	81	83
1985	78	80
1986	-	83
1987	-	77
1988	-	74
1989	-	77
1990	-	85
1991	-	86
1992	-	82
1973-79 average	85	-
1980-85 average	81	-
1973-85 average	83	-
1980-85 average	-	82
1985-92 average	-	81
1980-92 average	-	81

Source: Census of Production (NI and UK); Hitchens, Wagner and Birnie (1990).

Table 2.2 presents a series of comparative GVA per head for total manufacturing for 1973-85 based on the 1968 Standard Industrial Classification (SIC) and also our more recent data for 1980-92 on the SIC 1980. It was not attempted to harmonise the two industrial classifications for the years 1986-92.

Total manufacturing comparative productivity between Northern Ireland and Great Britain during the 1980-92 period was quite volatile since it varied from a low of 74 in 1988 to highs of 86 in 1981 and 1991. It was perhaps notable that the low of 74 in 1988 corresponded to the later part of the long 1980s upswing in the UK economy and the high of 86 to the bottom of the recession in 1991 (i.e. there is some evidence that in recent years in relative terms Northern Ireland manufacturing is counter-cyclical with respect to the general trade cycle in the UK such that in relative terms Northern Ireland manufacturing does best when output in Great Britain is most depressed (NIEC, 1993b)). The main point to stress is that there was no clear trend of convergence; i.e. no clear pattern of Northern Ireland narrowing the gap on Great Britain.

Although the two series are not directly comparable it is significant that if successive periods of years are taken using either system of SIC the average of comparative productivities has dropped over time.

The two main conclusions derived from the total manufacturing data, variability and a lack of any clear trend of divergence or convergence, are also confirmed at the broad sectoral (i.e. two digit) level of disaggregation (Birnie and Hitchens, 1996).

In the rest of this section numbers in parenthesis refer to the two-digit industries of the 1980 Standard Industrial Classification (SIC). Metal manufacturing (22) experienced large fluctuations though its productivity level remained below that in Great Britain. In extraction of minerals not elsewhere specified (23) productivity remained below the Great Britain level and declined further. Productivity levels in manufacture of non-metallic mineral products (24) had been above those in Great Britain until the mid-1980s but then stabilised at a level below Great Britain. Levels in chemicals (25) initially rose to overtake those in Great Britain and then in the later part of the period declined so that Northern Ireland again fell short of Great Britain. In man-made fibres (26) productivity levels usually exceeded those in Great Britain but the scale of fluctuation was large.

In some cases in the engineering industries (e.g. manufacture of metal goods not elsewhere specified (31), mechanical engineering (32) and electrical and electronic engineering (34)) productivity levels fluctuated around a level below that of Great Britain. In manufacture of office machinery and data processing equipment (33) there was some convergence towards the Great Britain level albeit the productivity shortfall remained substantial (in this case given the small absolute size of output in Northern Ireland these estimates may be especially unreliable because of the effects of rounding). The productivity level in motor vehicles and parts (35) was very variable but usually fell short of that in Great Britain. There was a substantial productivity shortfall relative to Great Britain in other transport equipment (36) although Northern Ireland's comparative performance did improve during the second half of the period. In instrument engineering (37) Northern Ireland levels fluctuated above and below the Great Britain level during 1980-91 but then fell very substantially in 1992.

Along with man-made fibres, food, drink and tobacco (41/42) was the only broadly defined sector where Northern Ireland productivity levels exceeded those in Great Britain in almost every year. There was some variability (albeit, much less than in the case of man-made fibres).

In most of the remaining industries Northern Ireland productivity remained below the Great Britain level throughout 1980-92, usually by between 10 and 20 per cent. Rubber and plastics (48) provides an exception in that levels usually exceeded those in Great Britain.

From the point of view of our consideration of the prospects for the Northern Ireland economy within the EU it is important to stress that the implication of this sectoral analysis for policy is not an optimistic one. At least during the 1980-92 period, using the most up-to-date production census data which is available, there was little evidence of Northern Ireland productivity convergence towards Great Britain levels across a range of industries. During 1982-93 the real growth of GVA in Northern Ireland was only 3.8 per cent per annum compared to 4.9 per cent on average for the UK and rates of 5.0, 6.8 and 3.8 per cent for England, Scotland and Wales respectively (NIEC, 1998c). The next section examines whether this conclusion is reversed when we consider comparative performance over a longer time span.

Northern Ireland Long-Run Manufacturing Productivity Performance, 1912 to 1992

Having considered the 1980-92 productivity trends we now attempt to place these into the perspective of long-run data using the historical data for 1912-92 contained in Table 2.3.

Perhaps the most striking conclusion is that the extent of long-run productivity convergence between Northern Ireland and Great Britain total manufacturing has been very limited. Productivity levels of around four-fifths of Great Britain on average in 1980-92 were not very different from those achieved in 1949 (71 per cent) and 1912 (72 per cent). Thus, to the extent that the active (and expensive) industrial policy in Northern Ireland from the late 1950s onwards was trying to achieve parity with Great Britain levels of productivity it failed by a large margin.

A slightly more favourable picture is given by the trends in some of the individual industries. In mechanical engineering, electrical engineering, instrument engineering, metal goods, other manufacturing, textiles and clothing there was a clear improvement. In textiles and clothing this was concentrated from the mid-1970s onwards. However, in metal goods and the three sectors of engineering an improvement began earlier but then seemed to have been exhausted by the 1960s. In contrast to these industries which improved relative to Great Britain, in only one was there a clear downwards trend; shipbuilding. Some other industries experienced stability in their comparative productivity; leather, bricks etc., timber and furniture, and paper etc. Food, drink and tobacco was a rather volatile performer which in some years lay above the Great Britain productivity level. Man-made fibres is a relatively new industry and so the scope to identify historical trends in man-made fibres is limited but it can be noted that since its emergence it has consistently shown higher productivity levels in Northern Ireland than in Great Britain.

At the sectoral level we could conclude that there is not much evidence of sustained convergence towards Great Britain productivity levels. The upwards movement in comparative productivity in mechanical, electrical and instrument engineering which was concentrated in the years between the end of the Second World War and the 1960s may well have been attributable to a once and for all gain arising from inward investment. Unfortunately, such inward investment and structural change failed to set off a process of continued convergence.[2]

Table 2.3 Northern Ireland net output per head[a], 1912 to 1992 (NI/GB, GB = 100)

	1912	1924	1930	1935	1949	1958	1963-73 average	1973-85 average	1980-92 average
Total manufacturing	72[b]	68	62	62	71	68	84	81	82
Food, drink & tobacco	97	75	61	81	80	87	106	96	104
Tobacco	-	-	-	-	-	84	-	78	123
Chemicals	75	47	75	73	88	-	121	77	58
Metals	-	-	-	-	-	41	72	87	78
Mechanical engineering	54	-	-	77	65	77	89	89	85
Instrument engineering	53	-	-	-	91	89	76	88	67
Electrical engineering	54	-	-	-	75	83	79	76	85
Transport equipment	-	-	-	-	-	-	67	61	72
Shipbuilding	109	-	-	-	-	-	59	41	35
Aerospace	-	-	-	-	-	-	70	86	62
Metal goods	78	-	-	-	-	91	89	94	86
Textiles	70	73	72	71	67	71	73	89	96
Man-made fibres	-	-	-	-	-	-	138	120	195
Leather & fur	-	-	-	-	-	84	78	78	89
Clothing & footwear	-	70	63	63	70	71	71	80	81
Bricks, pottery, glass & cement	-	108	118	107	93	91	95	100	87
Timber & furniture	100	78	73	73	73	95	80	91	85
Paper & printing	87	77	78	75	73	75	79	82	77
Other manufacturing	-	-	-	-	-	60	80	103	126[c] 85[d]

[a] Some of the data shown (especially for the more disaggregated industries) are the results of estimations e.g. tobacco for 1973-85 and shipbuilding and aircraft for 1963-73 and 1973-85, and in these cases the results for a single year, either 1968 or 1984, were used to represent the average for the whole period. The results for each Census year used the system of industrial classification which was then current. The exceptions to this were the years 1980-85 where the data were re-estimated on the basis of the 1968 SIC. The new definition in the 1980 SIC had the effect of improving Northern Ireland's total manufacturing comparative productivity. The 1980-92 average figures were, however, based on the 1980 SIC.
[b] Result estimated. Data were available for Northern Ireland in 1912 for sectors which represented 87 per cent of total manufacturing net output in 1924. The remaining sectors, clothing and drink and tobacco were estimated; the former using the 1924 relationship between sales and net output, the latter using the 1912-24 growth of nominal net output in food. The Great Britain total manufacturing net output per head was available for 1907. This was up-dated to 1912 using volume indices in Broadberry (1992) which implied productivity growth of 1.6 per cent to which was added 9 per cent for price increases (no producer price index was available so the average of the indices of food and clothing prices was used (Phelps-Brown, 1973)).
[c] Processing of rubber and plastics.
[d] Other manufacturing industries.

Source: As Table 2.2.

Apart from attempting to characterise industries according to the trends in their comparative productivity level there is also the question of whether there is any pattern in the ranking of industries according to their comparative productivities; are the industries which do well relative to Great Britain always the same (and are the ones which do badly always the same)? This question is given force by the findings of international comparisons which have shown stability in the pattern of UK/USA industrial comparative productivities (Rostas, 1948; Paige and Bombach, 1958; Smith, Hitchens and Davies, 1982). In fact, there is only limited stability in the pattern of Northern Ireland comparative productivities.

Table 2.3 shows how, for example, in 1912 shipbuilding, timber etc. and food, drink and tobacco were at the top of the ranking by comparative productivity, whereas mechanical, electrical and instrument engineering came in the last three positions of this ranking. In later years timber etc. stayed in the top half of the rankings (though in 1980-92 only just) whereas shipbuilding fell so as to become one of Northern Ireland's worst performers in comparative terms. Bricks etc. had a high ranking in both

1958 (second), 1973-85 (third) and 1980-92 (sixth). Food, drink and tobacco had a position in the top half of the ranking in every year. New industrial development was illustrated by man-made fibres having the best comparative productivities in 1963-73, 1973-85 and 1980-92 and also by chemicals (second in the ranking in 1973-85) and aerospace (third in the ranking in 1973-85). It was however notable that chemicals and aerospace were almost at the bottom in 1980-92 which indicates the fragility of their earlier success with respect to comparative performance. Textiles and clothing occupied a fairly stable position in the bottom half of the rankings.

The marked instability in terms of ranking by comparative productivity level was indicative of the impact on relative performance of shifts in demand and inward investment. This instability also implies that during 1912-92 Northern Ireland manufacturing had not yet been able to achieve sustained convergence across a range of industries. A further implication for policy is that the comparative productivity data does not suggest much evidence of successful clusters within Northern Ireland manufacturing. One international study has suggested that clusters of competitive firms are rarely if ever engineered by a deliberate government policy (Enright, 1994).

Our analysis has so far indicated a lack of productivity convergence for total manufacturing or broad sectors in either 1980-92 or 1912-92.

Explanations of Comparative Manufacturing Productivity

The previous sections of this Chapter have shown that the manufacturing sector in Northern Ireland is characterised by relatively low productivity and, by implication, a weak competitiveness performance (Gorecki, 1997). In this section we outline briefly possible explanations of relatively low productivity. Hitchens and Birnie (1994) consider in some detail the explanatory factors which might underlie Northern Ireland and Republic of Ireland manufacturing performance and the next Chapter will review those factors which possibly impact on the performance of more than one sector including manufacturing.

Lower Capital Intensity?

Other things being equal, output per head rises with the amount of capital available per worker. The available statistical evidence, such as relative rates of investment per head and estimates of capital stock per worker, casts doubt on the proposition that capital intensity (i.e. the amount of capital such as machinery available per worker) in Northern Ireland or Republic of Ireland manufacturing is lower than that in the UK (Harris, 1983; Henry, 1989; Hitchens, Wagner and Birnie, 1990; Hitchens and Birnie, 1993, 1994). Moreover, matched plant studies indicate that sample firms in Northern Ireland and the Republic of Ireland were not disadvantaged relative to Great Britain counterparts in terms of the availability of capital and were often at no disadvantage relative to West German, Dutch or Danish counterparts (Hood and Young, 1983; Hitchens and O'Farrell, 1987, 1988a, 1988b; Hitchens and Birnie, 1993) which might have been expected to have levels of capital intensity greater than the UK average (O'Mahony, 1993).

Inadequate Size of Plants and Firms?

Standard economic theory notes the importance of economies of scale. As output rises the average cost of producing each unit of that output often drops. Could a lack of such economies of scale explain the weak competitiveness performance of Northern Ireland manufacturing? In 1985 the average (median by employment) plant size in Northern Ireland manufacturing was only about 70 per cent of that in Great Britain and in the Republic of Ireland about 60 per cent. As two small economies it is not surprising that firms in Northern Ireland and the Republic of Ireland are also generally relatively small and that there is a small representation of medium and larger sized enterprises (those employing more than 499 persons). Table 2.4 uses 1993 data to compare the average plant size in Northern Ireland with the UK average and the Republic of Ireland.

Table 2.4 Firm size in Northern Ireland, the United Kingdom and the Republic of Ireland, 1993[a]

	Mean employment sizes			Mean net output sizes (£'000s)		
Industries[b]	NI	UK	ROI	NI	UK	ROI
Food, beverages & tobacco	32	52	57	890.5	1,932.2	4,171.0
Textile products	66	22	47	1,120.0	413.3	830.6
Leather products	45	33	28	755.0	658.2	515.4
Wood products	9	8	19	222.0	196.4	429.9
Paper & printing	18	13	34	538.5	547.2	2,547.7
Chemical & man-made fibres	31	52	68	1,626.1	3,267.7	11,095.3
Rubber & plastic products	30	29	36	1,028.6	923.6	1,181.8
Other non-metallic mineral products	13	21	33	397.4	705.0	1,252.4
Metals and fabricated metal products	8	15	23	204.7	444.9	657.3
Other machinery & equipment	22	25	39	548.2	754.7	1,237.6
Electrical & optical equipment	38	32	88	991.3	1,034.9	5,115.3
Transport equipment	105	73	62	2,380.0	2,796.6	1,470.3
Other manufactures n.e.s.	8	10	25	157.1	240.4	871.7
Total manufacturing shown[c]	25	23	-	637.0	780.8	-
Manufacturing	26	-	44	694.7	-	2,579.6

[a] Republic of Ireland data is for establishments in 1993 (only for those employing three or more persons) and net output values converted to £ using the average market exchange rate. The Northern Ireland and UK net output per establishment is an approximation; output data for 1993 was divided by the number of units in 1996.

[b] Industries defined using the two letter groupings of the SIC 1992 (i.e. DA to DN) and then roughly matched to the two digit groups of the NACE (i.e. 15 to 37).

[c] Excludes data for Division 16 - manufacture of tobacco products (which was also excluded from food, beverages and tobacco), and sub-section DF - manufacture of coke, refined petroleum products and nuclear fuel.

Source: Data supplied by Department of Economic Development (Northern Ireland) and quoted by Bradley and McCartan (1998) plus the Republic of Ireland, Census of Industrial Production 1993.

The data presented relates to mean values and therefore gives no indication of the extent to which the distribution of plants by size is skewed in the three areas. In terms of average employment size, Northern Ireland is not at much of a size disadvantage relative to the UK average. Indeed, in only six of the 13 subsectors did the average employment size in the UK as a whole exceed the Northern Ireland value. However, the UK average plant appears larger than that in Northern Ireland in terms of net output per local unit (nine of the 13 subsectors). Similarly, in nine of the 13 subsectors Northern Ireland plant sizes were smaller than the Republic of Ireland average in terms of net output. (The Northern Ireland-UK data on the one hand, and the Republic of Ireland on the other, are not on strictly comparable bases and so the comparisons should be treated with caution but they are at least indicative that the Republic of Ireland now has some very large plants and these are often the consequence of inward investment).

In fact, as Table 2.5 illustrates, the Republic of Ireland now has three manufacturing companies placed within the list of Europe's top 500 public limited companies (PLCs) by market capitalisation whereas Northern Ireland has none (the origin of a company being determined by the location of it headquarters). Once adjustment is made for relative national/regional population size it would appear that if Northern Ireland had been as successful as the Republic of Ireland or any of the small Continental economies illustrated in Table 2.5, then it would have had at least one representative in Europe's top 500. If it had been as successful as either Norway or Switzerland there would have been three.

Table 2.5 Development of large PLCs; Northern Ireland compared to small European economies, 1997 (number of companies within Europe's top 500 by market capitalisation, end of 1997)

	Manufacturing	Non-manufacturing[a]	Total	Total if NI's pop.[b]
Northern Ireland	0	0	0	0.0
Republic of Ireland	3	0	3	1.3
Switzerland	5	8	13	3.1
Belgium	4	7	11	1.8
Denmark	2	3	5	1.6
Sweden	6	3	9	1.7
Austria	2	3	5	1.0
Netherlands	7	4	11	1.2
Norway	5	4	9	3.4

[a] For example, utilities, financial, extractive, transport and extractive industries.
[b] Actual total adjusted downwards according to the ratio between the size of that country's population and that of Northern Ireland.

Source: Financial Times (1998, January 22).

The Republic of Ireland has indeed been somewhat more successful that Northern Ireland in developing big, indigenously controlled PLCs but there are two things to note about this. First, it is a recent development driven by overseas acquisitions on the part of two companies (CRH and Jefferson Smurfit) as well as the merger between, and transformation to PLC status, of various dairy co-operatives (building up the Kerry Group). Second, the Republic of Ireland does not yet appear to have been successful in developing any very large non-manufacturing companies. Table 2.6 shows that even by the standards of the Republic of Ireland, Northern Ireland locally controlled manufacturing firms have relatively small turnovers (and one of the companies on this list, Shorts, has in recent years become part of an international group, whilst the second ranking company, Powercreen, at the time of writing, is still recovering from a major financial crisis).

Table 2.6 Largest (by turnover) Northern Ireland-controlled manufacturing firms compared to the three largest Republic of Ireland companies, 1996/97 (taken from Europe's top 500 by capitalisation)

	Turnover ($, m.)*	Sector
NI company		
Shorts	660	Aerospace
Power-screen	490	Engineering
United Dairy Farmers	420	Dairying
Lamont	200	Textiles
Desmond & Sons	190	Clothing
Harland & Wolff	190	Shipbuilding
Boxmore	140	Packaging
O'Kane Poultry	130	Meat processing
Brett Martin	90	Building products
Galen	60	Pharmaceuticals
ROI company		
Jefferson Smurfit	3,800	Packaging
CRH	3,600	Materials
Kerry Group	1,800	Dairying

* Using the September 1997 average market exchange rate.

Source: Belfast Telegraph (1998, February 18).

What is much less clear is the extent of any impact on performance arising from a lesser scope for economies of scale. What is certain is that other factors intervene to determine performance. Hitchens, Wagner and Birnie (1990) show that in certain sectors in Northern Ireland plant size exceeded that of Great Britain but productivity was lower. On the other hand, the very high productivity of the foreign owned firms in the Republic of Ireland, e.g. in pharmaceuticals, has been attained in spite of relatively small plant sizes (Birnie, 1994).

O'Malley (1989) attributed the relatively weak performance of the Republic of Ireland indigenous manufacturing in large part to the disadvantage of being a late-starter to the industrialisation process though in a case such as Denmark the switch from agriculture to manufacturing did not occur many decades before the Republic of Ireland, and in Finland successful industrialisation has largely been a post-Second World War phenomenon. However, the late starter thesis is in any case not appropriate to Northern Ireland where the disadvantage seems to be rather those of an early starter where the large regional firms of the nineteenth century were established in the 'wrong' sectors from a twentieth century point of view.

NESC (1992a) widened consideration beyond simply the timing of industrialisation to argue that the Republic of Ireland has a poorly developed national system of innovation. In other words, social, cultural, institutional and economic forces have restricted the development of entrepreneurship, risk-taking and application of technology and one consequence of this has been that homespun companies have not grown to any great size. The very low rates of R&D activity in Northern Ireland (NIEC, 1993a) suggest a problem of a similar nature. It is also worth considering whether, even if other factors had permitted the growth of larger indigenous firms in the Irish economies, this would have been constrained by a lack of managerial talent capable of co-ordinating the activities of large internationally orientated companies. International matched plant comparisons and exchange visits by managers in Northern Ireland and West Germany to factories in the other country provided some hints of this (Hitchens, Wagner and Birnie, 1991; Hitchens and Birnie, 1993). Such a position is unsurprising to the extent that the general post-war British track record in providing strategic management in activities such as car manufacturing, electrical engineering and aerospace has been less than exemplary (albeit, with some signs of improvement since the 1980s). Thus Northern Ireland and the Republic of Ireland may share in this difficulty in devising and maintaining corporate and product strategies appropriate to technologically complex manufacturing activities. The general conclusion should probably be that relative size is as much a consequence of performance as the reverse.

Disadvantaged in Terms of Vocational Education, Training, Skills and Experience?

During the last twenty years much of the research on the so-called 'British disease' in UK manufacturing has focussed on a weak skills base, especially on the shop-floor, and consequent deficiencies in terms of labour force flexibility and competence. In terms of the percentage of the manufacturing labour force with a degree in Northern Ireland the proportion is only about half that for the UK as a whole (Hitchens and Birnie, 1993, 1994). Northern Ireland, the Republic of Ireland and the UK are similar in having a much higher proportion of workers without either an intermediate vocational qualification (e.g. apprenticeship training) or higher qualification than is the case in West Germany, the Netherlands or France. In one respect, this may be too favourable a picture of Northern Ireland and the Republic of Ireland's relative position given that the size of the industrial base is so small. When stocks and flows of qualifications are standardised by population size their relative position weakens.

A recent study by the authors (Hitchens, Birnie, McGowan, Cottica and Triebswetter, 1998) suggests that in two branches of food processing, a sector where Northern Ireland is usually considered to have competitive advantages, the representation of certificated qualifications (i.e. degree, technical and craft-trained levels) fell behind not only West Germany but even south Italy (generally considered to be one of the weakest peripheral regions within the EU).

Table 2.7 Percentage of workers with certificated qualifications, Northern Ireland, Republic of Ireland, south Italy and West Germany, 1995

	Dairying*	Meat Processing*
Northern Ireland	10	12
Republic of Ireland	9	9
south Italy	12	19
West Germany	49	17

* The sample sizes were about 6 firms in each sector in each area.

Source: Hitchens, Birnie, McGowan, Cottica and Triebswetter (1998).

There are two ways in which training and skills could impact on performance. Firstly, the representation of vocational skills on shop-floor can effect physical productivity, i.e. the volume of output per operative, through better attention to detail and the superior utilisation of machinery and materials. This was strongly implied by the matched plant comparisons between the UK and West Germany (Daly, Hitchens and Wagner, 1985; Steedman and Wagner, 1987, 1989) and also by the inter-regional and international comparisons involving Northern Ireland and the Republic of Ireland (Hitchens and O'Farrell, 1987, 1988a, 1988b; Hitchens, Wagner and Birnie, 1990; Hitchens and Birnie, 1993, 1994). Secondly, and this may be even more important in complex factor product activities, the skills and experience of management may determine the quality component of productivity (i.e. the value added component of individual products). In any case it is not simply a matter of differences in paper qualifications, though there is some evidence that continental firms benefit from a greater representation of managers with a background in engineering. Northern Ireland and Republic of Ireland managers have been shown to be relatively cautious in their product and corporate strategies with, for example, a preference in clothing and textiles for long runs of standardised products rather than flexible production, and in food processing a concentration on commodity products as opposed to final consumer items (Hitchens, Wagner and Birnie, 1991; Hitchens and Birnie, 1993). Roper (1997) argues manufacturing as a whole has been slow to adopt the principles of New Competition; R&D, extensive inter-firm collaboration and flexible and adaptable organisational forms.

Inefficiency Created by High Rates of Government Subsidy?

Both Irish economies have long been characterised by relatively high rates of government subsidies. This may have had negative impact on comparative productivity performance in the case of manufacturing.

Table 2.8 demonstrates that during the early 1990s there was a major reduction (of the order of one-half in real terms) in levels of industrial development spending in Northern Ireland (Chapter 8 considers the thinking behind the industrial strategy introduced at the start of the 1990s and also attempts to evaluate this new approach based on 'competitiveness'). This reduction was, however, part of a general European trend and the decline in Great Britain was even greater (Martin and Tyler, 1992). By implication, in relative terms manufacturing in Northern Ireland continued to be heavily subsidised Hamilton (1996) noted that

> ...it is still difficult, if not impossible, to learn of an industrial investment project in Northern Ireland that has not received assistance of some sort and the average rates of assistance stood at almost 26 per cent in the mid-1990s and in a significant number of cases much higher.

Table 2.8 Annual average net grant expenditure per head in various EU regions (£, 1992 prices)

	1986-92	1992
Italy	215.1	-
Luxembourg	76.1	112.5
Northern Ireland	60.6	29.1
Republic of Ireland*	43.7	30.6
Greece (1986-88)	37.5	-
Belgium	36.5	24.6
Portugal (1989-92)	33.5	27.7
Germany (1986-91)	31.9	-
Great Britain	29.8	13.5
Netherlands	21.2	17.6
Spain (1986-91)	13.7	-
Denmark (1986-90)	6.8	-
France (1986-91)	5.4	-

* Not including any imputed value for the tax concessions.

Source: Yuill, Allen, Bachtler, Clement and Wishlade (1995).

By way of comparison, rates of grant assistance of manufacturing plants in Scotland under the Regional Selective Assistance scheme averaged 15.5 per cent over the period 1990/91 to 1992/93 (Scottish Office, 1993).

On a wider definition of assistance (i.e. all public grant aiding to investment, enterprise development and industrial land and factories but excluding expenditure on training) the industrial development budget in Northern Ireland in the early to mid-1990s per head of the workforce was still over three times higher than that in Scotland and more than twice as high as that in Wales (Office for National Statistics, 1996). In the Republic of Ireland actual rates of grant aid paid as a percentage fixed asset investment declined from over 38 per cent in 1986 (O'Malley,

Kennedy and O'Donnell, 1992) to 22.7 per cent in 1992 (Yuill et al., 1995).

One inference which could be drawn is that firms have become dependent on subsidies as a substitute for the gains to profitability that might otherwise have arisen through productivity and efficiency improvements. Roper (1993) provides some evidence of this. By implication there might be some gains to competitiveness following on from a further reduction of grant payments in Northern Ireland and the Republic of Ireland.

Failure of Policy to Promote a Strong Indigenous Sector?

Even if the hypothesis that subsidies led to increased inefficiency is rejected it still seems to be the case that industrial policy in both Northern Ireland and the Republic of Ireland has failed to achieve positive benefits commensurate with its cost.

As was noted in the previous section, measured by rates of grant payments, industrial policy in Northern Ireland has if anything proved even more expensive than that in the Republic of Ireland (Hitchens, Wagner and Birnie, 1990). However, in contrast to the Republic of Ireland, as a region within the UK the taxpayers of Northern Ireland have not had to shoulder this burden.

Is it possible to go a stage further and argue that not only was policy unsuccessful but it actually represented a negative institutional effect on economic performance? For example, the inward investment policies pursued by both Northern Ireland and the Republic of Ireland during 1950s to 1980s may have involved some displacement of locally owned firms (though it is not clear how far this happened as a consequence of a discriminating effect of the package of industrial incentives or as an inevitable result of the inefficiencies of the indigenous sector).

There are several ways in which such displacement could have happened. First, grant assisted inward investment firms may have been able to undercut local firms on cost and hence put them out of business. There are some reasons to be sceptical as to whether this was a big problem, the established local firms were more likely to be serving a local regional market and inward investor a national/international one and so they would not be in direct competition. Second, and this may have been more significant, the arrival of inward investors may have bid up wages thereby raising labour costs which may have been a blow to some marginal firms.

A further problem in the case of Republic of Ireland industrial policy, which does not have a counterpart in the Northern Ireland case, has been the harmful indirect effects of the relatively low rate of tax on corporate profits (10 per cent). This is of particular interest because it is sometimes suggested that Northern Ireland should reduce its corporate profit tax rate down from the UK level (about 30 per cent) towards the much lower Republic of Ireland rate. The counterpart of relatively low taxation on capital has necessarily been a relatively high rate of taxation on labour (Culliton, 1992).

As a number of reviews of industrial policy have recognised, the authorities in both Irish economies are still searching for a set of policies which would successfully promote a strong indigenous sector (Telesis, 1982; DED, 1990; Culliton, 1992) and inward investment by international firms has traditionally received the lion's share of attention and resources from the policy makers. Some recognition of the need to give more priority to indigenous enterprise has been given by the recent administrative shake-up of development agencies in the Republic of Ireland ('Employment through Enterprise - The Response of the Government to the Moriarty Task Force on the Implementation of the Culliton Report and Government of Ireland' (1993)) whereby two separate agencies are charged to develop home industry and promote inward investment. This begs the question whether some similar institutional reform in Northern Ireland in relation to the relative responsibilities of the Department of Economic Development, Industrial Development Board and Local Enterprise Development Unit might be desirable.

What is less clear is how far the lack of priority given to the indigenous sector contributed to the lack of competitiveness evidenced in home firms (Hitchens and O'Farrell, 1987; Hitchens, Wagner and Birnie, 1990). Given certain supply side weaknesses in locally owned firms (e.g. with respect to human capital as described above) it is possible that a different institutional set up which gives more priority to the indigenous sector would of itself have achieved little. Nevertheless, it is probably the case that policy makers over-emphasised the externally owned sector. This may have been because the competitiveness problems of indigenous firms were poorly understood. The use of grants to attract outside companies was therefore an easier option than attempting to reverse the specific competitiveness failures of local firms.

The Effects of the Troubles?

Political instability and the violence since 1969 has certainly had a direct and negative effect on employment and investment (Rowthorn and Wayne, 1988; Gudgin, Hart, Fagg, Keegan and D'Arcy, 1989). Moreover, the Troubles have probably had a sizeable though indirect effect in so far as they have impacted on institutions (see below). Such effects have certainly been greater in the case of Northern Ireland than the Republic of Ireland (see also Chapter 7).

The System of Decision Making and Administration in Northern Ireland?

It is probable that the situation of over-subsidisation previously referred to would not have been allowed to develop in the absence of the Troubles since 1969. Until comparatively recently successive British governments were led to regard Northern Ireland as a special case where public spending should be exempt from the constraints imposed elsewhere in the UK. Thus workers and managers in Northern Ireland manufacturing firms were encouraged to regard privileged access to continuing subsidy support as an entitlement. Privatisation was delayed during most of the 1980s as industry in Northern Ireland was shielded from the full rigours of so-called 'Thatcherism', and with the 'shock' thus weakened the consequent growth in productivity was also more limited than the 'productivity miracle' experienced elsewhere in the UK.[3]

The administrative framework which has developed in Northern Ireland may also have handicapped economic performance in the sense that the policy makers in Belfast (i.e. mainly civil servants) are only weakly subject to any controls which would otherwise cause failed policies to be adjusted. For example, the Direct Rule system of political decision making from London has meant that locally elected politicians have only minimal input into economic policy making. Though it is not clear whether the local political parties, unionist, nationalist and others, if they had been in a position of power post-1972, and if they had been provided with fiscal resources from London comparable to those which did arrive under Direct Rule, would have followed policies which differed from the policy of expensive and heavy subsidisation which has been tried and found wanting. (It remains to be seen whether the outcome of the inter-party talks which began in June 1996 and concluded in April 1998 will be such as to permit some responsibility for economic policy making to be returned to local representatives.)[4]

While the administrators of policy in the civil service and agencies are officially accountable to the team of government ministers sent over from London (though these politicians have probably less reason to be sensitive to the local electorate than their counterparts in Scotland and Wales) it is debatable how much control arises given the short-term nature of appointments and general preoccupation with constitutional issues. Neither were the local policy makers likely to feel strongly accountable to either the Treasury or Westminster as a whole. The sums of public money being spent in Northern Ireland are large relative to the Northern Ireland economy but sufficiently small relative to the total UK economy to pass by relatively unnoticed especially given the resigned apathy towards Northern Ireland amongst much of the British political establishment.

From 1993 onwards this situation may have begun to change. There were indications of a growing feeling in Great Britain that the fiscal transfer from London to Belfast, i.e. the Subvention to Northern Ireland (£3.5 billion in 1993), would have to share in the sacrifices which reduction of the UK's PSBR of £50 billion would require. There were even suggestions that greater financial stringency in Northern Ireland would in some sense promote greater realism and hence, so the argument went, a greater willingness to accept political accommodation (Financial Times, 1993, October 28; O'Leary, Lyne, Marshall and Rowthorn, 1993; The Times, 1993, October 27). It is therefore notable that during 1997/98, 1998/99 and 1999/2000 there is a planned cut in real terms in Northern Ireland public spending while small growth is planned for Great Britain (NIEC, 1997b). This remains the case notwithstanding some small increases in the Northern Ireland spending block during the first two Labour Budgets (July 1997 and March 1998). Government ministers have also emphasised that as the allocation of spending to law and order had to be increased again during 1995/96, given a period of instability, this has had negative implications for, for example, the educational and labour market budgets.

Recent publications of the Northern Ireland Economic Council have given prominence to governance as a determinant of the Province's economic performance. For example, NIEC (1996) argued that the quality of policy would be improved if there were some scope for decisions about regional spending and taxation levels to be decoupled from national UK policies. It remains unclear, however, whether this could be achieved without damage to the 'parity' principle whereby, notwithstanding the relative narrow local tax base, the Province should not be disadvantaged with respect to local standards of public services. A second reason to qualify the NIEC proposal is that it is unlikely a local decision making body could be given much power to increase levels of public spending when the ratio of public spending to regional GDP is already about one and a half times the UK average and there is a considerable fiscal Subvention from the national Exchequer. In principle such a body could be empowered to change both government spending and tax levels at the margin in the same way that the Scottish devolved Parliament is to be able to raise income tax rates by up to three percentage points above the UK average if is so wishes. The multi-Party agreement of 10 April 1998 made no provision for any independent tax raising powers in the local Assembly. Dunford and Hudson (1996) noted that in a number of 'successful' continental European regions, and especially the Abruzzo region of southern Italy, there was a high degree of trust and consensus amongst the political elite. This has obviously so far been lacking in the Northern Ireland case.

One particular institutional impact of the Troubles is that in contrast to Great Britain Northern Ireland has very strong legal machinery prohibiting discrimination in employment (the Northern Ireland legislation relates largely to discrimination on grounds of religion whereas in Great Britain the emphasis is on race Teague (1993); Bew, Patterson and Teague (1997)). To the extent that there are differences between the levels and types of training and skills of Protestants and Catholics in Northern Ireland (Osborne, 1985; Wilson, 1989) then a legal imperative on firms to employ the religious groups in proportion to the composition of the local population, while some would judge this politically desirable, introduces a constraint on operation which could impair efficiency. If, however, discrimination were simply an economically 'irrational' act whereby an employer chose one religion over another when all the potential employees on offer were alike in every other way then the legal constraint would not have any efficiency cost. (Teague (1993) provides an innovative attempt to apply recent economic analysis of the working of labour markets to the particulars of discrimination in Northern Ireland.)

Further efficiency costs of the Fair Employment law include the opportunity cost in terms of managerial time and the restrictions on the ability of the unemployed in Northern Ireland to use informal methods and networks to apply for jobs. In a recent survey of long-term unemployed, Borooah and Forsythe (1997) found that only 11.9 per cent of those in Northern Ireland who had been successful in finding a job had used direct applications and/or informal approaches to employers but in Scotland (24.6 per cent) and south east England (19.5 per cent) the proportions were almost twice as high.

The Existence of the Border Has Itself Been a Major Cause of Under-Performance?

Is the division of the island between two political units itself a cause of under-performance through the associated loss of economies of scale and the increase in various costs? This factor has been stressed by Rowthorn and Wayne (1988). Munck (1993) went so far as to argue partition itself has been, '... the greatest impediment to the development of Ireland during this century'. In Chapter 7 we imply an answer to this question by identifying those areas where there could be gains to co-operation. If the gains to co-operation are implied to be large then this might suggest that the partition of Ireland into two separate political units in 1921 was a major handicap on subsequent economic performance. (Our approach is the reverse of that in the Cecchini Report (1988) where the costs of a so-called 'non-Europe' were first identified and then it was argued these indicated the scale of likely benefits arising from the Single European Market.)

The general conclusion to be drawn from such a consideration of the effect of the border on the economic performance of the Irish economies is that the impact is not likely to have been large though it is possible to identify certain ways in which co-operation and joint administration of economic policy between the two economies could today lead to certain gains (see Chapter 7). This implies that a lack of co-operation or common administration in the past has led to certain economic costs though the indications are that these were not large. If partition had not occurred and a united Ireland post-1921 had pursued a different set of policies (e.g. as regards subsidising manufacturing and industrial policy) then there could have been large gains arising from this different institutional set up. However, it is not clear that a different political arrangement was a necessary condition for the adoption of alternative and more effective economic policies or that it would have made those policies more likely. Moreover, the counterfactual as to what Northern Ireland's economic performance would have been post-1921 as part of a united Ireland rather than the UK is extremely complex (e.g. levels of public spending would probably have been lower without the transfer of resources from the Exchequer in London though it could be argued that this would lead to long-term benefits to the extent that greater economic realism and self-reliance were produced). If Northern Ireland and the Republic of Ireland had different economic interests in the 1920s and 1930s (e.g. in favour of free trade with Great Britain in the case of Northern Ireland, or for protection from Great Britain in the case of the Republic of Ireland) then partition may have brought economic benefits to the extent that it allowed each Irish economy to adopt the most suitable policy (O'Malley, 1985).

Notes

1. World trade in commercial services was only $1,000 billion in 1992, as against $3,640 billion of merchandise trade, of which $2,650 billion was in manufactures (Financial Times, 1994, February 24). Northern Ireland manufactured 'exports', i.e. inclusive of sales to Great Britain, in 1990 were estimated to have been about £4 billion (Scott and O'Reilly, 1992) and it is unlikely that exports from all other sources (e.g. agriculture and services) amounted to any more than £1 billion (at that time extra-regional agricultural sales were only about £500 million).

Table 2.9 The extent of openness of the Northern Ireland economy, comparisons with the United Kingdom and Scotland

	External sales ratio	Export ratio*
United Kingdom (1996)	-	28.9
Northern Ireland (1994)	39.7	20.0
Scotland (1989)	62.4	25.4

* All sales beyond the UK whereas external sales are sales beyond the confines of the region. There is a small downward bias in the Northern Ireland figure relative to Scotland and the UK in that the Northern Ireland data is confined to manufacturing and does not allow for exports from other sectors.

Source: McGregor, Swales and Yin (1998).

2. According to some recent theories of economic growth (so-called endogenous growth theories) growth can lead to more growth in a sort of cumulative process (Romer, 1986; Lucas, 1988). The key empirical issue is whether in fact there are increasing returns to investment in either physical or human capital and whether such investment creates favourable externalities (e.g. if firm A invests in training not only does this raise productivity in A but also the productivity of firm B with which it has linkages). Crafts (1993) reviews the evidence from Continental and UK data and is sceptical as to the extent of such endogenous growth. Certainle post-war Northern Ireland does not seem to provide a strong example of it.
3. The structure of incentives facing politicians in Northern Ireland as well as the nature of the socio-economic interest groups which had been formed may partly explain the delayed introduction of Thatcherism to Northern Ireland. A Queen's University research student, Graham Brownlow, is currently attempting to apply the insights of public choice theory to help explain the development of economic policy in Northern Ireland and the Republic of Ireland.
4. All the political parties in Northern Ireland have to varying degrees backed policies of high levels of public spending along with fairly interventionist industrial and agricultural policies. Given that they have had almost no responsibility for the raising of the tax revenues to fund such policies it could be argued that they have had little incentive to do otherwise (for this and other reasons Gibson (1996), amongst others, has argued that any devolved settlement should include some degree of tax raising powers). Birnie (1998)

shows how both unionists and nationalists over the years have used claims about the working of the economy, and sometimes these positions have not been very soundly based, to bolster their case on the constitutional argument.

3 Sectoral Competitiveness: Agriculture, Business Services and Tourism

Introduction

The previous Chapter reviewed Northern Ireland's comparative performance with respect to manufacturing labour productivity and attempted to explain that performance. This Chapter outlines performance in a number of other sectors.

Table 3.1 illustrates the comparative productivity performance of Northern Ireland alongside that of the Republic of Ireland for those tradable non-manufacturing activities for which data were available. The Irish economies are compared to the UK average and also the standards of the highest productivity economy at the European and the world levels.

A more detailed consideration of the factors influencing performance at the sectoral level, including the tourism sector, is discussed. Although it was not possible to compare productivity levels in tourism, that sector also has been (or has the potential to become) an important contributor to total export levels from the two Irish economies.

Table 3.1 Northern Ireland (NI) and Republic of Ireland (ROI) comparative productivity in the non-manufacturing sectors

Sector	Year		as % of UK	as % of European leader	as % of World leader	Possible explanations
Agriculture	1985	NI	80	51	42	Land quality, farm size, capital, fertilisers and feeds, training
Agriculture	1985	ROI	77	49	41	Same as in NI
Railways	1991	NI	53	20	c. 5	Network size?, capital, subsidies (relatively small)
Railways	1991	ROI	97	37	c. 10	Same as in NI
Buses: urban/ suburban	1988	NI	< ROI	-	-	As in railways
Buses: urban/ suburban	1988	ROI	58	71	-	Same as in NI
Road freight	1987	NI	-	-	-	
Road freight	1987	ROI	30	16	-	Capital, roads?
Ports	1986	NI	137	-	-	Larne container roll-on/roll-off.
Ports	1986	ROI	89	< 50	-	Public ownership?, industrial relations?, low capacity utilisation.

Table 3.1 ctd...

Sector	Year		as % of UK	as % of European leader	as % of World leader	Possible explanations
Airlines		NI	No separate carriers	British Airways probably highest productivity European Airline	BA etc. < USA airlines	
Airlines	1989	ROI	42	42	c. 30	Ownership, protection, subsidies (high)
Airports	1988	NI	c. 80-90	-	-	?
Airports	1988	ROI	76	-	-	?
Tele-communications	1987	NI	no regional breakdown available on BT etc.	-	-	
Tele-communications	1987	ROI	55	23	23	Ownership? capital indicated higher than UK?
Banks	1985	NI	99	91	64	Technology, industrial relations? NOT branch size, along with UK relatively large

Table 3.1 ctd...

Sector	Year		as % of UK	as % of European leader	as % of World leader	Possible explanations
Banks	1985	ROI	43	40	28	Same as in NI
	1990-91		56	42	-	
Retail	1990	NI	93	70	-	
	1994		86	-		
Retail	1985	ROI	76	65	62	Shop type? Unit size?

Source: Mainly calculations by the authors (e.g. Birnie (1996)) based on a range of official statistics such as Commission of the European Communities (1993, 1994) and also previous international productivity comparisons (Baily, 1993). The NI comparative productivity in retail was a comparison of GDP per head (Cambridge Econometrics, 1997).

Agriculture and Food Processing

In 1973 agriculture on its own contributed about 8 per cent of the GDP of Northern Ireland but by 1996 this share had fallen to 5 per cent compared to 8 per cent in the Republic of Ireland and about 2 per cent in Great Britain (Davis, 1998). The agricultural workforce represented about 11 per cent of the total regional employment in 1973 and by 1996 this had fallen to 6 per cent (compared to 13 per cent in the Republic of Ireland and just over 2 per cent in Great Britain). Taking agriculture and food processing together, Table 3.2 shows the contribution of these activities to the Northern Ireland economy.

Table 3.2 Contribution of agriculture and food processing to the Northern Ireland economy, 1973 and 1996 (% of total)

	1973	1996
GDP	12	8
Employment	15	10

Source: DANI (1997), Davis (1998).

Agriculture still contributes a large proportion of the total exports of the Irish economies, one-quarter of total Republic of Ireland commodity exports in 1988. The exports of other primary products remain small. In 1991 agricultural exports were recorded as $5.86 billion compared to manufacturing exports of $16.9 billion and service exports of $5.57 billion (WEF, 1991). The proportion in the case of Northern Ireland would be smaller but still substantial Manufacturing exports beyond Northern Ireland in 1990 were estimated to have been about £4 billion (Scott and O'Reilly, 1992) while agricultural exports beyond Northern Ireland in 1991 were £548 million out of a total sectoral gross output of £882 million, and a large proportion of manufacturing export sales are derived from food processing. It is, however, unclear how much scope there is for further growth in the volume of exports. This is because of general oversupply of farming products throughout the EU and the recent renegotiation of the General Agreement on Tariffs and Trade (GATT) leading to the World Trade Organisation (WTO) and the 1992-95 MacSharry reform of the

Common Agricultural Policy (CAP) both of which imply that the rates of subsidy are likely to be reduced on Republic of Ireland and Northern Ireland food products as exports to non-European markets (NESC, 1992b). The European Commission's 'Agenda 2000' document in July 1997 proposes further reductions in price support levels as well as ceilings on the compensating direct payments to farmers.

Climatic conditions (mild and moist) mean that Northern Ireland probably has a comparative advantage in grass-based livestock activities. Dairying is indeed the largest single element at the farming and processing stages. Over 80 per cent of sectoral value added is derived from dairying, beef and sheepmeat (Davis, 1998). Potatoes now contribute only 2 per cent of the industry's output.

Table 3.3 Share of main products in final agricultural production, United Kingdom, Northern Ireland and the Republic of Ireland, 1995 (% in total final production)

	UK	NI	ROI
Cereals	16.3	1.6	5.5
Other crops	8.3	-	3.4
Fruit & vegetables	9.5	2.5	3.0
Milk	21.8	29.7	32.1
Cattle	15.1	33.6	37.6
Pigs	8.0	10.1	6.5
Eggs, poultry	9.9	11.7	4.0
Total of products shown	88.9	89.2	92.1

Source: Commission of the European Communities (1996).

Milk output roughly doubled during the first decade of EC membership but the imposition of milk quotas has meant that output has stayed more or less static at its 1984 level. The move to the European Single Market in 1992 helped to undermine the statutory monopoly position of the Milk Marketing Board, previously the sole purchaser of farm milk, and this scheme was brought to an end in 1995. It is unclear what the balance of effects on farmers and processors will be of this move towards a much freer market in the supply of raw milk.

The beef sector experienced decline throughout much of the 1970s (Davis, 1998).[1] The beef herd then expanded from 1987 until 1994. On 20 March 1996 the UK Minister of Health announced the possible link between consumption of beef and the disease CJE (human form of BSE). Domestic consumption levels fell by 30 per cent during the late spring of 1996 though much of this decline was subsequently reversed. However, these difficulties in the domestic market were followed by a world-wide ban on UK beef exports imposed by the EU's Council of Ministers. Previously, about one-half of Northern Ireland's beef output had been exported beyond the UK (indeed, of total annual UK exports of about £520 million in 1995 45 per cent derived from Northern Ireland).

Northern Ireland farmers and processors have claimed they have suffered unfair guilt by association with the rest of the UK. It is true that the incidence of BSE in Northern Ireland cattle has been much lower than in Great Britain, 1,769 cases (as of early 1998) amongst a herd of 1.6 million compared to more than 170,000 in the Great Britain herd of 11 million, i.e. a Great Britain rate of incidence about 14 times greater. This is perhaps attributable to the lower use of processed feeds and the easier traceability of individual animals in Northern Ireland. At the same time the Northern Ireland record appears much worse than either that of the Republic of Ireland or the rest of Europe: the number of confirmed cattle BSE cases were, for example, only 123 in the Republic of Ireland, 13 in France, four in Germany and two in Italy (Economist, 1996, March 30, April 6).

The UK government has adopted a policy of selectively slaughtering (i.e. mainly older cattle). This includes some of the cattle currently used on dairy farms (old and redundant dairy cattle would no longer be allowed to be slaughtered for human consumption as before). Thus the BSE crisis has had grave implications for dairying as well. To the extent that this cull was designed to restore consumer confidence within the UK it appears to have worked to a great extent. However, the EU remains to be convinced and at the time of writing the EU bans on most UK beef products remain in place.

At the same time, in March 1998 (The Times, 1998, March 5) the Council of Ministers did propose resumption of beef exports applying to deboned beef from cattle aged between six and 30 months which come from herds certified to have been free of BSE for eight years. Significantly, Northern Ireland is the only part of the UK which meets these stringent EU conditions because it has established a computerised system for tracking its cattle from birth. Other UK regions are now setting up such systems. Caskie, Davis and Papadas (1998) predict about 20 per cent of the jobs in the beef sector are under threat unless the Northern Ireland beef crisis can be resolved (i.e. several thousand jobs could be lost). Beef represented about one-third of Northern Ireland agricultural sales in the mid-1990s and supported 15-16,000 jobs in total. Another study suggested about one-quarter of these jobs could be under threat if the ban on beef exports is not removed (Financial Times, 1998, March 16).

Supply Side Constraints on Competitive Performance

As in the case of manufacturing, the productivity level in agriculture in Northern Ireland and the Republic of Ireland is substantially lower than the UK average. This is a longstanding phenomenon though there does appear to have been some variation in the relative position of Northern Ireland and the Republic of Ireland over time. Such a shortfall has often been attributed to the relatively small size of farms and hence a lack of economies of scale (Boyle, Kearney, McCarthy and Keane (1991) provide a detailed analysis of the extent of farm size economies of scale in the production of certain commodities). Table 3.4 presents data on comparative international productivity (net output per person in total employment) in agriculture and comparisons of average farm sizes (in hectares).

Whereas some of these results are now dated, the pattern of international productivity differences is not likely to have changed much since the mid-1970s and so conclusions can be drawn. More research is required to elucidate the connections between farm size and performance, and while Northern Ireland and Republic of Ireland farms may be small by UK standards this is not true within a wider EU perspective.[2] While the UK has substantially larger farm sizes and higher productivity than either Northern Ireland or the Republic of Ireland, the Netherlands, for example, manages to achieve even higher productivity in spite of even smaller farms.

Table 3.4 Comparative agricultural productivity, various years, and relative farm size, 1985

	Labour Productivity (as a per cent of the UK value, UK = 100)					Farm size (hectares, UK = 100)
	1938	1968	1975	1985	early/mid -1990s	1985
United Kingdom	100	100	100	100	100	100
Netherlands	-	98[a]	159	157	-	23
France	-	81[a]	78	91	-	41
Republic of Ireland	63	55	70[b]	77[b]	85[c]	35
West Germany	-	88[a]	57	59	-	25
Northern Ireland	50[b]	-	51[b]	80[b]	92[d]	37

[a] 1957-1960 compared to the UK (Hayami, Miller, Wade and Yamashita, 1971).
[b] Net output per head compared using relative prices of principal products (Birnie, 1994). The Northern Ireland estimate for 1938 was based on gross output per head then therefore should be regarded as only roughly comparable with the other comparisons. Ó'Gráda (1994) suggested that in the 1930s real agricultural productivity in the Republic of Ireland may have been up to 10 per cent greater than in Northern Ireland.
[c] Estimate for 1993 based on an updating of the benchmark measurement for 1985 using indices of employment and the volume of output.
[d] Estimate for 1994 uses GDP per head data from Cambridge Econometrics (1997) and makes no allowance for any difference in product price levels.

Source: As above and Hitchens and Birnie (1994) updated. Farm size data are from SOEC (1990), except for Northern Ireland which is from Spencer and Whittaker (1990). Labour productivity data are from van Ooststroom and Maddison (1984, 1993), except for Northern Ireland and the Republic of Ireland which are from Birnie (1997).

Apart from the size of farms, it has been argued that the predominance of owner-managed farms in Northern Ireland and the Republic of Ireland relative to the UK or the rest of the EU inhibits performance given that a high proportion of these farmers are old, under-qualified or unenterprising.

Unfortunately there is a lack of good data on the quality of the labour force compared to other regions and countries. Keenan (1977) found that only 16 per cent of farmers in the Republic of Ireland had completed any sort of post-primary education and only 2 per cent had studied for a year or more at an agricultural college. On the other hand, the stock of skills has been improving over time. NESC (1976) in its survey of new farm operators under 30 years of age between 1971 and 1975 found that 63 per cent had some form of post-primary education and 16 per cent had attended agricultural college. If there is any shortfall of skills this may be as much a problem of a lack of demand for those skills as a lack of training capacity. NESC (1979) argued that agricultural colleges in the Republic of Ireland were producing more trained persons than the farms were then absorbing. Less evidence is available as to the relative level of qualifications amongst the Northern Ireland farming labour force, however, the situation is unlikely to be much better than in the Republic of Ireland (DFP, 1993).

In addition to the relative farm size and training of the labour force, the comparative level of capital and other inputs could represent constraints upon performance. Birnie (1997) estimates that the capital stock per person in employment in Republic of Ireland agriculture was about 80 per cent of the level in the UK in 1985. Such a relatively low level of capital intensity would be consistent with the comparatively low level of labour productivity which has been indicated. However, Whittaker and Spencer (1986) suggest that capital intensity in Northern Ireland farming was considerably higher than the level in the Republic of Ireland in the late 1970s (perhaps more than twice as high). This would imply that capital intensity in Northern Ireland was at least as high as the UK average. Furness and Stainer (1981) conclude that there may have been over-investment in Northern Ireland agriculture and that higher mechanisation had not yet justified itself in terms of either output growth or widening of profit margins. The use of feeding stuffs per person in employment in the Republic of Ireland in 1985 has been estimated to be about one-half of the rate in the UK (Birnie, 1994). The intensity of use of feeds in Northern Ireland is likely to be higher than the Republic of Ireland reflecting the greater representation of intensive livestock activities (pigs, poultry and eggs, Spencer and Whittaker (1986)). In considering the usage of feeds it is worth noting that peripherality adds to the price of these inputs and therefore disadvantages Northern Ireland and Republic of

Ireland farms. A comparisons of the intensity of use of fertilisers in farming in the Republic of Ireland and UK suggests this is similar in the two areas (Birnie, 1997).

In summary, farming remains a significant player within the Northern Ireland economy. Unfortunately, both demand (e.g. the liberalisation of world trade in agriculture) and supply (e.g. small farms with under-trained farmers) factors imply it is also a weak and vulnerable sector where growth prospects are limited. Personal income levels are low (and had declined markedly during 1997/98) and it remains unclear how, if at all, these can be raised whilst at the same time realising certain other desirable objectives such as rural development and environmental protection. Dependency on subsidies exceeds that of even the manufacturing sector. Davis (1998) reckoned that in the period from 1991 to 1995 transfer payments averaged about one-half of total income from farming. Once the impact of price support is included Gudgin (1998) suggested that the total implicit subsidy for farming was about equal to the income earned in the sector (our own calculations would confirm this, see Chapter 5).[3] In the next section we consider the manufacturing and processing activities most closely linked to agriculture, i.e. the food processing sector.

Food Processing: Constraints on Competitiveness

Given likely demand side developments as the EU is forced to liberalise agricultural trade relative to the rest of the world the scope for quantitative expansion in agriculture is limited. There may be more scope, as Telesis (1982), Culliton (1992), and Government of Ireland (1993) have noted, for the Republic of Ireland food-related manufacturing industries to improve the value added of their products (either through engaging in further processing activities or by the supply advanced farming-related services). This probably also applies to Northern Ireland (DFP, 1993). The food, drink and tobacco branches of manufacturing represent one-fifth of total manufacturing employment in both Irish economies. Poultry meat represents one of the most rapidly growing major subsectors of food processing and Davis (1998) judges it the most successful in terms of product innovation. He attributes this to the fact that it has operated with minimum intervention and support under CAP over the last 25 years and has been forced to develop its international competitiveness in order to survive. The following constraints on food processing have been identified:

- Very low rates of R&D spending and a lack of innovational success (Maguire, 1979; Sectoral Development Committee, 1985; Hitchens and Birnie, 1993; NIEC, 1993a);
- Seasonality of supply of certain inputs (e.g. milk) is said to restrict the capability to provide retail consumer products on an all year basis (Hitchens and Birnie, 1993) though this constraint is less marked in the case of Northern Ireland than the Republic of Ireland;
- The home market in either Northern Ireland or the Republic of Ireland is small. This makes it harder for firms to develop marketing or retailing economies of scale;
- Even the largest Northern Ireland or the Republic of Ireland companies are usually relatively small operators within the context of the EU Single Market (though the Kerry Group, as shown in Table 2.5, is an exception). Hence, there is a lack of resources to establish brands in continental Europe (in the diary processing sector Davis (1998) identified substantial inefficiencies and the need for rationalisation);
- Peripherality and hence the penalty of higher transport costs both in terms of selling output and buying in certain imported inputs (e.g. feeds).

Fishing and Forestry Activities

In addition to whatever gains to output and employment may be attained in farming and food processing there may be some scope for growth in forestry and fishing. In both Irish economies these activities are probably underdeveloped relative to their potential in natural resource terms. Given the recent rapid growth in forestry and aquaculture (fish farming) in the Republic of Ireland (NESC, 1993b) there may be gains to Northern Ireland in learning from the Republic of Ireland in these activities.

Business/Producer Services

The opportunities and challenges posed by producer services (e.g. accountancy, marketing, designing, legal and research) are similar to those which characterise the banking and financial sector (Hitchens and Birnie, 1994). There are few strong indigenously owned companies and these operate within a very small home/local market. Producer services are of interest because they appear to have favourable growth prospects, i.e. through extra-regional exports they could generate growth in their own right (Marshall, 1988), and they are also considered as inputs to manufacturing. Therefore the price and non-price competitiveness of indigenous producer services suppliers may have an impact on the performance of the existing manufacturing firms and perhaps contribute to the attraction and retention of new firms (Marshall, 1982; Marquand, 1983; Damesick, 1986; Bailly and Maillet, 1988; Stabler and Howe, 1988; Hansen, 1990). There is some evidence that producer services, like financial services (Kinsella, 1992), are comparatively underdeveloped in Northern Ireland in quantitative terms given that business services in Northern Ireland represent only 0.8 per cent of total UK employment in this sector (total regional employment being 2 per cent of the UK total) in contrast to a greater than expected proportion, 58.8 per cent, in the South East region of the UK. Data on a comparable basis are not available for the Republic of Ireland. During the period 1981 to 1989 employment in the business services sector in Northern Ireland grew by only 79 per cent as compared to average UK growth of 171 per cent (Hitchens, O'Farrell and Conway, 1996a, 1996b). Growth in the Republic of Ireland was probably similar to the UK average (198 per cent during 1980-90 for a wider definition of business services i.e. categories 323, 329-333 from the Population Census).

Constraints on Business Service Competitive Performance

The following constraining factors are probably significant:

- Small home market;
- Small size of firms;
- Under-provision of certain items of equipment;
- Under-representation of higher skills;

- Lack of specialisation in the activities undertaken (especially in Northern Ireland).

In a comparison of samples of producer service firms (advertising, market research, graphic design, producer design and management consultancy) Hitchens, O'Farrell and Conway (1996a and 1996b) showed that those in the South East region of the UK had stronger employment growth during the period 1985/86 to 1990/91 than matched counterparts in Wales, Northern Ireland and the Republic of Ireland. Growth in the Republic of Ireland firms exceeded that of the businesses in Wales and Northern Ireland. Some of the firms in the South East were larger than their counterparts. When the comparisons were restricted to cases where the matched companies were of similar size average employment growth was roughly the same across the four areas. When the productivity of the companies was compared a similar pattern emerged, i.e. service companies in the South East had the highest productivity and they were followed by those in the Republic of Ireland, Wales and Northern Ireland (Table 3.5).

Table 3.5 Comparative business service labour productivity, 1991, value added per head, compared using exchange rates, (South East = 100)*

	South East	Republic of Ireland	Northern Ireland	Wales
Advertising	100	88	53	82
Market research	100	93	57	88
Graphic design	100	56	51	57
Product design	100	58	43	49
Management consultancy	100	70	46	71
Total sample	100	75 (75)	50 (53)	71

* Sample sizes were 46 (41), 40 (40), 44 (39) and 44 respectively. Numbers and results in parenthesis relate to matched comparisons with Northern Ireland where larger firms, with no counterparts in the Northern Ireland sample, were excluded from the samples for the other regions.

Source: Hitchens, O'Farrell and Conway (1996a).

It is notable that Northern Ireland business service productivity was only one-half of the South East level while the Republic of Ireland firms attained productivity levels of only about three-quarters of that of counterparts in the South East. In this case adjustment for firm size makes little difference to the results. An examination of the pattern of sales is of interest since this may also be indicative of competitive strength.

Table 3.6 Exports[a] as a percentage of total sales, sample business service companies, 1991

	South East	Republic of Ireland	Northern Ireland	Wales
Advertising	10 (24)	8 (9)	2 (0)	1 (18)
Market research	23 (34)	29 (13)	10 (18)	3 (38)
Graphic design	13 (18)	3 (10)	7 (3)	0 (25)
Product design	24 (47)	28 (43)	6 (1)	2 (9)
Management consultancy	28 (27)	14 (28)	3 (12)	0 (50)
Total sample	20 (29)	15[b] (18)	5[c] (7)	1 (30)

[a] Exports outside of the ROI or UK, extra regional sales within the UK are shown in parenthesis)
[b] Includes three percentage points of sales in Northern Ireland.
[c] Includes four percentage points of sales in the Republic of Ireland.

Source: As Table 3.5.

When exports proper are considered the same pattern of the South East and the Republic of Ireland leading Northern Ireland and Wales appears. Northern Ireland appears to have a small advantage relative to Wales though this disappears once the definition of exports is widened to include any sales outside of the region including those to other parts of the UK. Further indicators of the particular competitive weakness of the Northern Ireland companies were a relatively high dependence on public sector contracts (hitherto probably a relatively soft market; Clulow and Teague (1993)) and a smaller number of identified direct competitors.

In terms of the explanations of performance, the Northern Ireland and Republic of Ireland firms were more likely to complain about the lack of certain items of equipment. Degree or professional level qualifications were more likely (70 per cent) to be represented in the firms in the South East than in their counterparts in Northern Ireland (54 per cent) or the Republic of Ireland (50 per cent).

The performance of the producer services in fact overlaps with that of the financial sector broadly defined. Table 3.7 shows the comparatively small size of the financial sector in Northern Ireland compared to other regional economies.

Table 3.7 Percentage of total activity in the financial sector*, United Kingdom, Northern Ireland and other selected regions, 1995

	Employment (1995)	GDP (1994)
United Kingdom	16.7	27.1
Greater London	28.5	42.9
England	17.6	28.3
Wales	10.3	18.3
Scotland	14.4	21.6
Northern Ireland	7.9	18.1

* Defined as subsector J (financial intermediation, central and other banking, building societies, insurance and pension funds, other financial intermediation) and subsector K (real estate, renting of machinery and equipment, computer and related activities, research and development, other business activities- accounting, market research, architectural services, advertising, labour recruitment, investigation and security activities, industrial cleaning) of the SIC 1992.

Source: NIEC (1998c).

Table 3.8 shows that although the employment level started from a lower level, in proportional terms, than in Great Britain, growth during 1987 to 1996 kept pace with the rest of the UK.

Apart from some of the issues identified with respect to producer services (notably, the dependence on the small local market and hence the limited scope for specialisation), the growth of the financial services in Northern Ireland has probably been further constrained by the predominance of external ownership which has restricted the potential for extra-regional sales.

Table 3.8 Employment in financial services, Great Britain and Northern Ireland, 1987 to 1996

	Great Britain ('000s)			Northern Ireland ('000s)		
	J*	K*	J+K*	J*	K*	J+K*
1987	920	2,011	2,931	12.2	20.5	32.7
1988	996	2,140	3,136	12.6	21.7	34.3
1989	1,038	2,266	3,304	13.1	23.5	36.6
1990	1,047	2,392	3,439	13.4	26.3	39.7
1991	1,024	2,353	3,377	13.5	27.2	40.8
1992	991	2,363	3,354	14.1	27.8	41.9
1993	959	2,446	3,405	13.8	28.7	42.5
1994	965	2,455	3,420	13.7	29.9	43.6
1995	979	2,600	3,579	14.0	31.6	45.6
1996	974	2,753	3,727	13.5	32.8	46.4

* Subsectors of the SIC 1992 as defined as in Table 3.7.

Source: As Table 3.7

Tourism

Tourism already generates substantial employment in Northern Ireland, although to a smaller extent that in the Republic of Ireland. If allowances for tourist related employment in catering and recreation are made, employment in the Republic of Ireland has been rising towards 100,000 whilst that in Northern Ireland in the mid-1990s would have been about one-sixth of this. (The Northern Ireland Tourist Board estimates that jobs dependent on tourism grew from being 10,700 in 1993 to 12,500 in 1995 (NIEC, 1998c).) For the western economies as a whole tourism represents a tradable service which has a high income elasticity of demand and this provides the basis for the hope of further growth in the Irish economies in this sector.

There is still the question whether the existing infrastructure would be able to handle any further large scale increase in the number of tourists without very substantial negative externalities (e.g. congestion and pollution) which would undermine the attractiveness the destination. By implication, the Irish economies should perhaps seek a qualitative as opposed to quantitative upgrading of tourism (i.e. the same number of tourists would come but they would spend more money in Ireland). Northern Ireland, once again, has its own peculiar difficulty arising from the image problem created by the Troubles.

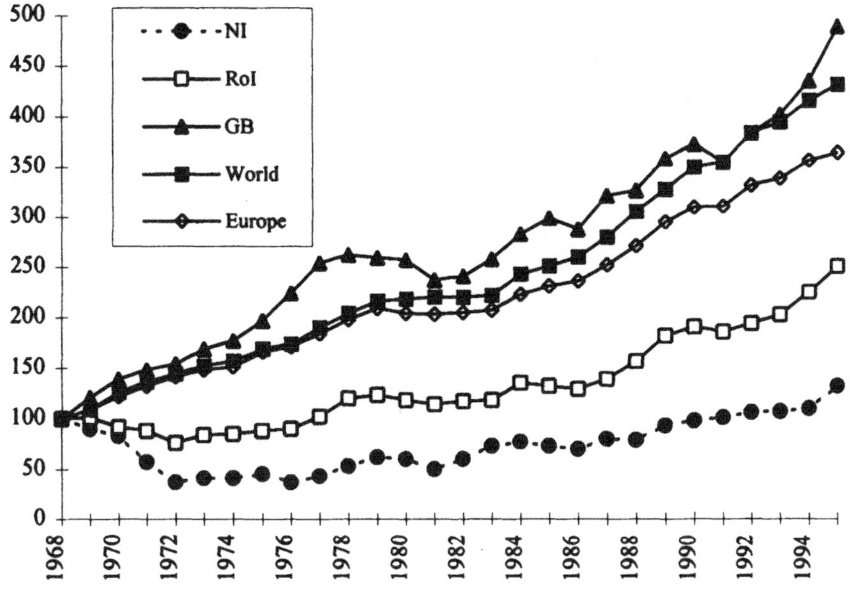

Figure 3.1 Growth in the number of visitors to Northern Ireland, Republic of Ireland, Great Britain, Europe and the World, 1968 to 1995 (1968 = 100)

Source: Constructed from data produced by the NIEC (NIEC, 1997a).

Figure 3.1 illustrates the relative depression in the growth in the numbers of visitors to Northern Ireland when compared to other areas between 1969 and 1995 and the up-turn during the 1994-95 ceasefires (there was a less favourable performance with the return to political uncertainty during 1995-97). It may be that it would be too costly for Northern Ireland to counteract this negative image within the mass tourist market. As a result the greatest pay-offs might be achieved by targeting efforts on specialist and high spending tourists.

Constraints on the Competitive Performance of Tourism

The following constraints can be identified:

- Peripheral location leading to relatively high access transport costs;
- Unattractive climate;
- Tourist facilities are often uncompetitive on price and non-price factors (see, for example, NIEC (1997a) on the hotel sector in Northern Ireland, and evidence of weakness with respect to foreign language skills (NITB, 1996));
- The expense of overseas marketing of Northern Ireland and Republic of Ireland destinations;
- The negative image of Northern Ireland arising from the Troubles.

It is notable that even if there was a permanent end to the violence the tourist industry in the two Irish economies would still be constrained by some of the factors listed above. There is also a very real possibility that there are already too many attractions chasing too few tourists (for example, the number of heritage centres had by 1994 already increased to about 25 in Northern Ireland and to around 50 in the Republic of Ireland and it has been argued that these are by their nature unlikely to get repeat visits even from residents of Ireland) with the implication that further public money spent on tourist development might simply displace activity away from existing attractions.

On the more optimistic side, as Table 3.9 shows, the increase in tourist numbers during the period of the ceasefires of 1994-95 outstripped expectations (NIEC, 1997a).

Table 3.9 Visitors and tourists coming to Northern Ireland, 1986 to 1997

	Total number of visitors ('000s)	Revenue (£ m.)	Holiday visitors only* ('000s)	Per cent of total
1986	824	81.8	106	13
1987	943	91.4	117	13
1988	930	97.0	125	14
1989	1,091	136.3	159	14
1990	1,153	153.0	222	19
1991	1,186	162.0	263	22
1992	1,254	162.0	247	20
1993	1,262	173.0	251	20
1994	1,294	183.0	275	21
1995	1,557	214.0	461	30
1996	1,429	206.0	296	21
1997	1,415	208.0	263	19

* Holiday visitors are defined as those closest to genuine tourist visitors as opposed to the 'Visiting Friends and Relatives' (VFRs) category.

Source: NIEC (1997a).

This suggests that if permanent peace were attained then the tourist industry might eventually face a new problem; the need to shift to a more 'sustainable' form of growth (i.e. smaller numbers of tourists each with higher spending levels) instead of having too many tourists each of which spend only small amounts of money.

Some Implications of the Productivity Analysis: Preliminary Conclusions on Competitiveness Performance

Taking manufacturing along with the other tradables sectors considered in this Chapter, perhaps the single most important conclusion is that productivity levels have been shown to be relatively low compared to Great Britain and indeed even more so relative to the USA and EU across a wide range of tradable sectors (i.e. those sectors which are most likely to be subject to external competition). Such levels are also relatively low in two further sectors not considered here; extractive industries and utilities i.e. water and electricity supply (Birnie, 1994; Pollitt, 1997). Manufacturing in the Republic of Ireland with its very high measured levels of productivity provides the most notable exception to this broad pattern (see Chapter 7). However, the sizeable Republic of Ireland productivity advantage relative to the UK can be entirely attributed to the foreign owned sector and in turn much of its recorded net output in fact derives from transfer pricing.

Relatively low industrial sector productivity levels contribute to the relatively low levels of living standards in the Irish economies, income per head still only about 80 per cent of the UK average albeit with rapid convergence on the part of the Republic of Ireland since 1986 (the Republic of Ireland/UK comparison being one of Gross *National* Product rather than Gross *Domestic* Product per head, the reasons for this choice of definitions of national income are given in Chapter 7). Admittedly, in the Republic of Ireland case a much larger part of this shortfall is immediately explained by the relatively low proportion of the population in work as opposed to the low productivity of those in work. However, low productivity and poor standards of international competitiveness may themselves contribute to the small number who are economically active. (Incidently, the fact that Republic of Ireland productivity levels in a range of sectors - farming, mining and quarrying, utilities, indigenous manufacturing, producer services, transport, telecommunications and postal services (Birnie, 1996) - might serve as some confirmation of recent questioning of the reliability or meaningfulness of national accounts measures which was noted in Chapter 1 (see also Chapter 7). Republic of Ireland GDP/GNP is not as large as it is indicated and some of the post-1986 growth may indeed be 'phantom' (Murphy, 1994, 1996) and attributable to the manipulation and exaggeration of measured profits in multinational branch plants as part of the transfer pricing phenomenon.)

Case by case consideration of the sectors suggest that certain standard economic explanations play a role in explaining the productivity shortfall, capital intensity and size (either of the plant, firm or home market). We have shown elsewhere that the productivity gaps are longstanding and in many cases present since partition and perhaps before (Hitchens and Birnie, 1994; Birnie and Hitchens, 1998). This might suggest that the role of the Troubles in Northern Ireland has been to slow down any convergence which might otherwise have occurred (e.g. in manufacturing). Notwithstanding some claims to the contrary (New Ireland Forum, 1984; Munck, 1993) there is no convincing evidence to suggest that partition itself had a sufficiently large dislocative effect to explain much of the productivity shortfall from the 1920s onwards.

Human capital (sometimes associated with R&D inputs) has been much favoured as a key explanatory variable in the new theories of economic growth (Romer, 1986; Lucas, 1988) and significantly policy makers in both Belfast and Dublin now officially recognise the role of education and training. Much emphasis has been given to the merits of the German 'dual' system of apprenticeship training (Hitchens, Wagner and Birnie, 1990; Culliton, 1992; Hitchens and Birnie, 1993; NESC, 1993b; Roper and Hoffman, 1993). However, it would be unwise to recommend that the Irish economies should simply copy Germany. The German model itself now seems to be in trouble (the supply of apprentices has declined as young Germans have decided to choose academic education as opposed to the vocational track). It is also questionable whether the German model can be transferred in part. Would Northern Ireland and the Republic of Ireland also have to replicate the German approach to industrial banking and trade unions, and is this at all realistic?[4] Northern Ireland and the Republic of Ireland already have a higher participation rate of young people in tertiary education than Great Britain, i.e. they have moved close to the American system of mass higher education. Soskice (1993) has argued that there are certain productivity advantages from the USA approach (it promotes higher productivity in information technology-intensive service activities) so perhaps it is the American rather than German model which is appropriate to the Irish economies (though, it might be doubted whether the American approach would be compatible with membership of any European Monetary Union because of the associated movement towards a system of high labour costs and heavy labour market regulation, see also Chapter 4 and Chapter 5, and it could also be asked whether the American approach tends to generate an unacceptable degree of poverty and inequality?).

The international literature has recognised that the absence of competitive pressure exerts a powerful negative influence on comparative productivity levels (Davies and Caves, 1987; McKinsey, 1993). In Northern Ireland and the Republic of Ireland substantial state aids are likely to have contributed to relatively low productivity levels in manufacturing, agriculture, utilities and parts of transport. However, official recognition has recently been given to the priority which should be given to measures which raise both comparative productivity and GDP per capita (Moriarty, 1993; NESC, 1993b; DED, 1990, 1995; DTI, 1995). Is this new policy emphasis working?

In Northern Ireland there have been problems operationalising the post-1990 'competitiveness strategy' (see Chapter 8 for a more detailed consideration). For example, the industrial development agencies are struggling to produce workable definitions and indicators of a competitive firm. The most recent document (DED, 1995) argued that some two-thirds of the remaining Northern Ireland productivity gap relative to Great Britain was caused by smaller plant size or a disadvantageous structural mix of activities. If this is true it would still be complacent not to ask why Northern Ireland continues to be characterised by such disadvantages.[5]

Notes

1. One reason for the earlier difficulties of the Northern Ireland meat sector was the working of the EU's 'green money system'. Under CAP EU support prices are set in ECUs. If prices in each of the EU states had tracked market exchange rates throughout the period since 1973 then at various periods this would have generated substantial instability in retail prices and farm incomes. In order to prevent this from happening a system of exchange rates peculiar to farm products were developed.

   During the late 1970s sterling had declined against the Continental currencies. However, in order to protect consumers from increased prices, the UK government was unwilling to devalue the green rate by anything like enough to bridge the gap between it and the market exchange rate. At times, therefore, there were very wide gaps between the market and green rates of between 25 and 30 per cent. The Republic of Ireland government, in contrast, was much more inclined towards the farming lobby and so did not allow such gaps to develop between its green and market exchange rates. The implication was that in the late 1970s a large gap opened up between the green price for farm products in the Republic and the lower prices being paid in the UK. The EC introduced a scheme of Monetary Compensation Amounts (MCAs) (a system of taxes or subsidies on cross-border exports) to try to remove any incentive which such gaps provided for cross-border trade within Europe. In practice, however, the MCAs could be easily avoided through smuggling (Davis, 1998). In one fortnight in 1976 virtually all of the cattle marketed in Northern Ireland 'disappeared' to south of the border. For obvious reasons, the absence of a land frontier with another EU member state, no other UK region suffered from problems on this scale.

As is often the case, one form of intervention in the market led to distortions which required further interventions to attempt to compensate and so on. During the late 1970s the UK government provided subsidy payments of about £30-40 million to support Northern Ireland meat processors.

The divergence between market and green exchange rates is now much smaller. This meant that Northern Ireland farmers enjoyed a windfall as the pound sterling depreciated by about 20 per cent after its exit from the Exchange Rate Mechanism of the European Monetary System in 1992. These gains were then reversed during 1997 and early 1998 as the pound sterling rose back to its 1992 levels against the Continental currencies.

2. The mid-1990s farm size statistics are shown in Table 3.10.

Table 3.10 Average size of farming holdings (hectares), mid-1990s

Northern Ireland	35
Republic of Ireland	29
Great Britain	70
EU 12 average	15

Source: DANI (1997), Davis (1998).

About 61 per cent of cattle and sheep farms are classified as 'very small' compared with about 40 per cent in Great Britain. Dairy herds have about 47 cows on average compared to 70 in Britain.

3. Hindley and Howe (1996) note the OECD estimation that for the EU as a whole in 1994/95 total transfers to farmers (both in terms of direct subsidy and price support) were 49 per cent of gross output. This implies a back of the envelope calculation but a still roughly correct way of indicating the scale of support for Northern Ireland agriculture. According to Northern Ireland Statistics and Research Agency (1997) total farming gross output in 1995 was estimated as £1191.8 million and 49 per cent of this would have been £584 million. This compared to total income for farming of only £338.2 million.
4. In other words, the working of the German training system may necessarily be embedded in the German social system. Fukuyama (1995) argues that a critical component of German economic success has been a high degree of trust between economic agents (e.g. large firms, regional governments and banks) which enable them to co-operate and so internalise externalities.
5. In the case of the Republic of Ireland the question is whether the good intentions of Culliton (1992) regarding tax reform and introduction of more

competition in various sectors (e.g. energy, telecoms and transport) are being fulfilled. Progress so far has been slow and some have attributed this to rent-seeking and various administrative/political factors; i.e. there is considerable power in vested interest groups which oppose policy reforms (Barrett, 1995).

4 General Influences on the Competitiveness of the Northern Ireland Economy

Summary

This Chapter supplements the sectoral reviews of the previous Chapters and considers a number of factors which are likely to have a general influence on competitiveness.

Transport Costs

These have often been cited as a disadvantage facing Northern Ireland firms exporting to Great Britain or further afield. There have been a number of attempts to measure the scale of such a cost disadvantage. For example, PEIDA (1984) used survey evidence and concluded that Northern Ireland firms faced costs which were on average 1-2 per cent higher than those in Great Britain (as a percentage of total turnover value) given the need to ferry goods across the Irish Sea and then drive to markets in England. Similarly, Hitchens, Wagner and Birnie (1990) used Census of Production data to show a similar difference in cost levels.

The NIERC (1992) survey of exports founds that almost half of manufacturing firms surveyed reported transport costs as a problem. In the 1996 Reward Regional Survey goods and services purchased in Northern Ireland were 3.1 per cent more expensive than those bought in Great Britain. A 1987 study (PPRU, 1987) reported that transport costs in Northern Ireland manufacturing firms were two-fifths greater than those in firms operating in the South East region of the UK (as a proportion of gross output) and accounted for 4.2 per cent of gross output compared to only 2.6 per cent in counterpart Scottish firms.

In other words, as a proportion of total gross output the disadvantage was not a large one. Admittedly, with value added typically being around

30-40 per cent of total gross output the impact of transport costs on value added would be greater. At the same time, given that wages in Northern Ireland are on average substantially lower than in Great Britain this would more than compensate for the impact of higher transport costs.

NIEC (1994) demonstrated that both in terms of frequency and charges international air and sea links and connections to Northern Ireland were relatively favourable. At the same time, the necessity to make an air or sea trip between Northern Ireland and Great Britain introduces uncertainty and the need to build in some contingency allowance (for connections) into travel times.

Peripherality

Whilst the direct impact of geographical location through higher transport costs may have been exaggerated, it seems likely that Northern Ireland has been disadvantaged by a broader problem of peripherality. To the extent that Northern Ireland firms are dependent on the local market (see Table 6.1) they are then relying on a small market which is cut off from the main population centres of both Great Britain and the EU.

The logistical difficulties of organising successful marketing arrangements across either the Irish Sea or English Channel imply that such firms will find it difficult to break into the wider markets and perhaps especially sub-supply activities (i.e. small firms supplying materials and inputs to larger international firms DFP (1993)). Both because of the physical isolation and also because, as already shown in Chapter 1, levels of prosperity lag behind other regions and countries, the fundamental problem of peripherality is that the Northern Ireland market is one which lags behind the leaders.

This could produce a vicious circle, because Northern Ireland is relatively less prosperous this makes it more difficult for Northern Ireland companies to design and fashion up-to-date products and services and this in turn hinders competitiveness and hence the attainment of further prosperity in the future. The peripherality problem also interacts with the labour market. Being on the edge of both the UK and the EU, Northern Ireland has so far had relatively small in-flows of population from the outside. Adverse labour market conditions have also meant that Northern Ireland has shared the general Irish characteristic of substantial outward migration. In recent decades the Troubles have clearly had a strong 'push' influence on migration and a relatively high proportion of those leaving have had above average levels of educational attainment.

Energy Charges

During the 1970s and early 1980s unit electricity charges to industry were roughly one-fifth higher in Northern Ireland than in Great Britain (Hitchens, Wagner and Birnie, 1990). By the mid-1990s this gap had if anything widened.

Table 4.1 Electricity prices in Northern Ireland relative to England and Wales, 1990/91-1995/96 (Ratio NI/E&W, based on unit prices at standard loads for different types of consumer)

	1990/ 1991	1991/ 1992	1992/ 1993	1993/ 1994	1994/ 1995	1995/ 1996
Domestic	1.04	1.02	1.04	1.09	1.09	1.19
Non-domestic	1.08	1.06	1.08	1.12	1.08	1.17
Medium sized firms	1.06	0.99	0.98	1.14	1.27	1.37
Large firms	1.01	0.96	0.94	1.06	1.07	1.15

Source: Pollitt (1997) based on data from the Centre for the Study of Regulated Industries.

At the same time, and notwithstanding the public alarm and political protest as to relatively high electricity prices in Northern Ireland, it is important to note that energy costs are typically only a small proportion of total industrial costs, in manufacturing usually about 2 per cent of total sales value. This would imply that the impact of the price 'wedge' between Northern Ireland and the rest of the UK would be relatively small (this argument is similar to that already made about transport costs). Moreover, the UK is somewhere in the middle of western economies with respect to electricity charges in industry. For example, a manufacturing firm in either Germany or Japan is likely to be paying as much for electricity as its Northern Ireland counterpart. It would be true that certain industrial activities which have very high usages of electricity are unlikely to locate in Northern Ireland.

Labour Costs

A longstanding feature of the Northern Ireland economy has been that the average level of wages and salaries has been substantially less than that in Great Britain. Between the 1950s and mid-1980s, however, this gap narrowed such that in manufacturing male manual wages moved up from being about 70 per cent of the Great Britain level to about 90 per cent of that level. Since the mid-1980s relative wage levels have moved down again.

Table 4.2 Average gross weekly earnings for adult full-time male employees, United Kingdom average, Northern Ireland and the South East (UK = 100)

	1971	1979	1989	1996
United Kingdom	100	100	100	100
Northern Ireland	88	90	86	84
South East	109	107	116	117

Source: Gudgin (1997).

Such changes should imply an increase in the relative cost competitiveness of Northern Ireland manufacturing and this may indeed be a partial explanation as to why manufacturing output growth has exceeded that in Great Britain since 1988. We have already shown that there was little improvement in Northern Ireland's comparative labour productivity in manufacturing between 1980 and 1992 and so the implication is that most of the increase in cost competitiveness came through this decline in relative labour costs. Table 4.3 shows relative wage levels in various economies.

Table 4.3 Comparative hourly total labour costs*, Northern Ireland compared to industrial and Newly Industrialised Countries, 1985 and 1995 (USA $, at market exchange rates)

	1985	1995
Northern Ireland	5.55	11.00
Germany	9.60	31.88
Japan	6.34	23.66
France	7.52	19.34
USA	13.01	17.20
Italy	7.63	16.48
Canada	10.94	16.03
Australia	8.20	14.40
Britain	6.27	13.77
Spain	4.66	12.70
South Korea	1.23	7.40
Singapore	2.47	7.28
Taiwan	1.50	5.82
Hong Kong	1.73	4.82
Brazil	1.30	4.28
Chile	1.87	3.63
Poland	-	2.09
Hungary	-	1.70
Argentina	0.67	1.67
Malaysia	1.08	1.59
Mexico	1.59	1.51
Czech Republic	-	1.30
Philippines	0.64	0.71
Russia	-	0.60
Thailand	0.49	0.46
Indonesia	0.22	0.30
China	0.19	0.25
India	0.35	0.25
Indonesia	0.22	0.30
China	0.19	0.25
India	0.35	0.25

* Includes non-wage costs to employer such as insurance schemes. Results for Northern Ireland estimated using the NI/UK relationship for male average weekly earnings in manufacturing. (In the absence of NI data on total annual hours it was

assumed that these were the same as the UK average. The proportional non-wage 'add-on' in NI and the UK are similar.)

Source: Morgan Stanley quoted in Economist (1996, November 2); PPRU (1986), CSO (1987) and ONS (1996).

It is important to stress that within the western world Northern Ireland, like the UK as a whole, is now a relatively low wage economy (this is especially true when comparison is made with the more expensive labour locations within the EU such as Germany). At the same time, average wage levels remain substantially higher than those in the Newly Industrialised Countries such as those in the Far East and many times higher than those in Third World economies. Northern Ireland labour costs are also substantially higher than those in the former communist eastern European economies which are now converting to the market system (see also Chapter 6). By implication, it would be shortsighted to rely on further reductions in Northern Ireland's relative level of labour costs as a strategy to promote competitiveness. In any case the minimum wage which will be introduced in 1999 will almost certainly be set a national rate ('It will be a single rate that will apply to all regions, sectors and sizes of firms'; Margaret Beckett, President of the Board of Trade, quoted in RSA (1998a)). This will, in effect, put a floor under Northern Ireland wage levels preventing any further reduction relative to Great Britain (NIEC, 1998a).

Size of Markets

Northern Ireland firms have a substantial degree of dependence on the local, provincial market (NIERC, 1992). About one-third of total manufacturing output is sold within Northern Ireland (see Table 6.1). This implies that some Northern Ireland firms (especially the smaller and medium sized ones) are largely dependent on what is a very small market. This in turn partly explains why Northern Ireland firms and factories are typically smaller than their counterparts in either Great Britain or continental EU (see Tables 2.5 and 2.6). Lack of size is often argued to produce certain economic disadvantages (fewer economies of scale are realised). At the same time, the relatively successful industrial performance of a number of Europe's smaller economies (e.g. Finland,

Sweden, Denmark and Switzerland) suggests that given the right corporate strategies, such as concentration on market niches, these advantages can be overcome (Hitchens, Wagner and Birnie, 1990).

Dependence on Branch Plants

Table 4.4 shows that historically Northern Ireland manufacturing has been more dependent on branch plants of foreign firms than has been the case for industry in Great Britain.

Table 4.4 Relative importance of foreign owned manufacturing plants in Northern Ireland and Great Britain (% of all manufacturing)

	Gross value added		Employment		Investment	
	NI	GB	NI	GB	NI	GB
1973	31.2	14.3	17.9	10.6	33.3	15.1
1979	30.0	20.3	22.7	13.9	37.4	21.2
1981	30.1	18.1	21.5	14.7	42.7	25.1
1983	19.6	18.6	16.3	14.5	35.7	22.7
1984	27.7	19.6	18.1	14.1	26.3	20.2
1985	18.2	18.1	13.5	13.6	20.4	21.1
1986	21.2	16.9	13.5	12.7	26.7	19.5
1987	26.4	17.8	13.2	12.8	34.0	20.1
1988	22.8	17.7	12.6	12.9	17.3	20.9
1989	27.6	20.5	12.2	14.7	23.4	26.8
1990	33.2	21.4	19.9	15.9	40.9	26.6
1991	38.7	21.2	21.8	17.0	42.2	33.2
1992	38.1	23.0	22.1	17.8	43.9	31.2

Source: Authors' calculations based on Census of Production.

This fact was sometimes held to partly explain the prevalence in Northern Ireland of 'production platforms', i.e. basic production facilities with few of the functions, such as R&D, marketing and higher management, which generate higher levels of value added (Harris, 1991). It is certainly true that industry has been characterised by relatively low rates of spending on R&D (total R&D spending in Northern Ireland in the early 1990s was equivalent to only 0.5 per cent of regional GDP whereas in the UK as a whole, and in the major western economies, the rate of spending was about 2 per cent, NIEC (1993a)). However, as Table 4.4 also shows, since the late 1980s the multinational sector in Northern Ireland first declined in relative size and then increased substantially so it is less likely that a 'branch plant syndrome' can be used to explain the relative weakness of manufacturing. In fact, as Table 4.5 demonstrates, in the mid-1990s Northern Ireland was by no means unique in its degree of dependence on foreign owned firms.

Table 4.5 Share of foreign owned companies in total manufacturing investment, selected countries and regions of the United Kingdom, 1995

	Foreign share of manufacturing investment (%)
United Kingdom	31.8
Northern Ireland	23.2
Wales	36.0
Scotland	48.4
England	29.7
North East	47.5
South West	19.8

Source: NIEC (1998b) using Department of Trade and Industry (DTI) data.

Moreover, relative Northern Ireland indigenous firms, inward investment in Northern Ireland has been relatively intensive in R&D spending. A 1991 survey of Northern Ireland R&D indicated that externally owned firms were more likely to be spending on R&D, 46 per cent, compared to indigenous, 29 per cent (DFP, 1993).

The Troubles

The violence since 1969 and the consequent political and economic instability is one obvious negative factor differentiating the local economy from both Great Britain and its southern counterpart. There can be no definitive estimate of the cost of the Troubles since to know this we would also have to know what would have happened over the last three decades in the absence of the Troubles. Nonetheless, various economists have estimated that if the employment growth trends present in the 1960s had continued unaltered by the Troubles into the 1970s and 1980s there would have been between 25,000 and 40,000 additional jobs in Northern Ireland in the early 1980s (Canning, Moore and Rhodes, 1987; Gudgin et al, 1989; Harris, 1991).

The direct and obvious cost imposed by the Troubles on Northern Ireland firms, e.g. in terms of property destroyed and expenses incurred in security measures, does not appear to have been large on average. At the same time, we cannot really know how much investment, whether by multinationals or local firms, would have occurred in the absence of the political uncertainty.

Perhaps the greatest effect on competitiveness has occurred through the labour market. For over a quarter of a century this has largely been closed off in terms of people coming in from either Great Britain or the Republic of Ireland or, indeed, further afield. Emigration, especially of relatively well qualified persons, has been encouraged. Thus local firms have often been restricted to a recruitment pool no larger than that of a single large English conurbation. To a great extent they have thus been denied access to people who have broader experience of international standards of excellence and best practice. Even when people of Northern Ireland origin have gone outside of the Province and got such experience the political situation has discouraged many of them from returning.

Attitudes to Work and Entrepreneurship

In the past Government ministers and representatives of the development agencies have claimed that one competitive advantage which the Northern Ireland economy does enjoy is something called 'the Northern Ireland work ethic'. In other words, not only are Northern Ireland workers relatively cheap to employ by the standards of their counterparts in the rest of the UK or mainland Europe but they are in some way more flexible and better workers. The next section questions whether levels of education and skills place Northern Ireland employees at any advantage relative to counterparts elsewhere in the EU.

Work attitudes and effort are not amenable to any straightforward and definitive measurement but comparative surveys of manufacturing firms (Hitchens, Wagner and Birnie, 1990; O'Farrell and Hitchens, 1989) failed to evidence any superiority in Northern Ireland work attitudes compared to counterpart plants in other regions within the British Isles. In these surveys, Northern Ireland managers were much more likely to complain about inflexibilities and resistance to higher throughput on the part of the workforce than their counterparts in West Germany were. We do know that on a matched industry-by-industry basis Northern Ireland had a higher strike rate than Great Britain during the late 1960s through to the early 1980s though thereafter the situation improved (Black, 1987).

During 1974-79 working days lost per 1,000 employees for the whole economy averaged 562 in Northern Ireland and 535 in Great Britain (Black, 1993). During 1987-90 these averages dropped to 111 in Northern Ireland and 149 in Great Britain (the rates for manufacturing alone were almost the same in the two areas, Northern Ireland at 195, Great Britain at 192).

Black (1993), using survey evidence taken mainly from the 1991 Social Attitudes Survey, found that Northern Ireland employees were more likely to be trade union members, 47 per cent compared to 37 per cent in Great Britain. In manufacturing, according to the 1989 British Social Attitudes Survey, employees were more likely to agree that 'workers need strong trade unions to protect their interest', 55 per cent compared to 38 per cent in Great Britain. Absenteeism was higher in Northern Ireland, as evidenced by the number of employees whose pay was affected by absence; 16 per cent compared to 10 per cent. Attitudes to work were less favourable in manufacturing (though not in the rest of the economy), those who said that they 'did the best that they could in work even if this interfered with the rest of their life' were 41 per cent in Northern Ireland but 58 per cent in Great Britain. At the same time, both Hitchens, Wagner and Birnie (1990) and Black (1993) suggested that Northern Ireland had inherited from its nineteenth century industrial past a relatively authoritarian style of management.

If there is any continuing problem in Northern Ireland industry with respect to work attitudes this may inter-relate to the impact of industrial policy (see Chapter 2). The longstanding policy of providing substantial and continuous subsidisation to many manufacturing firms may have been exploited by both management and workers (economists would term this the development of X-inefficiency).

Skills and Experience of Management and Labour Force

There is now a large body of research, associated especially with the National Institute of Economic and Social Research in London, which claims to evidence a link between a relatively low level of intermediate skills, i.e. vocational qualifications such as craft apprenticeships, and the comparatively low productivity level in UK manufacturing during the 1970s and 1980s (Prais, 1981; Daly, Hitchens and Wagner, 1985; Steedman and Wagner, 1987, 1989).

It now seems that this view provided a partial, though not complete explanation, of the 'British manufacturing disease'. It did not, for example, account for the rapid improvement in the UK comparative productivity performance since 1979 which has not been accompanied by any substantial improvement in levels of intermediate qualifications. Some other factors such as industrial relations, low levels of R&D spending and a narrowness of experience on the part of management were also contributory factors along with the dearth of craft skills.

For its part, Northern Ireland seems to have been a worse case of the 'British disease' with respect to training and skills. Figures 4.1 to 4.3 illustrate that the levels of qualifications were even lower than in Great Britain.

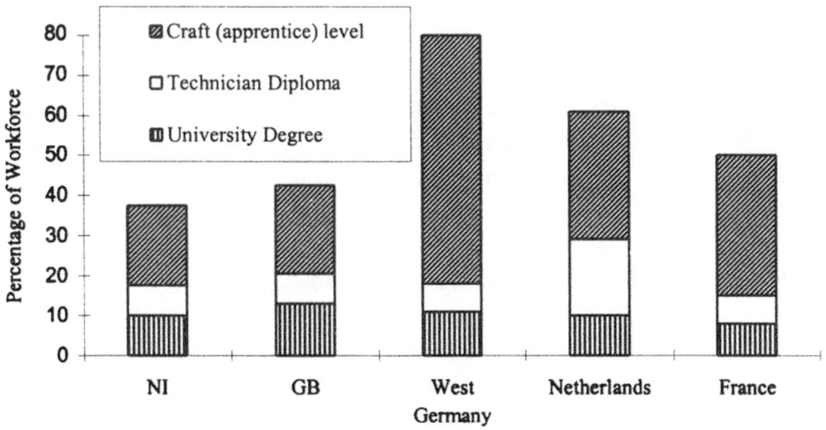

Figure 4.1 International comparisons of the level of vocational qualifications, early 1990s

Source: Various international official data sources quoted in T&EA (1996).

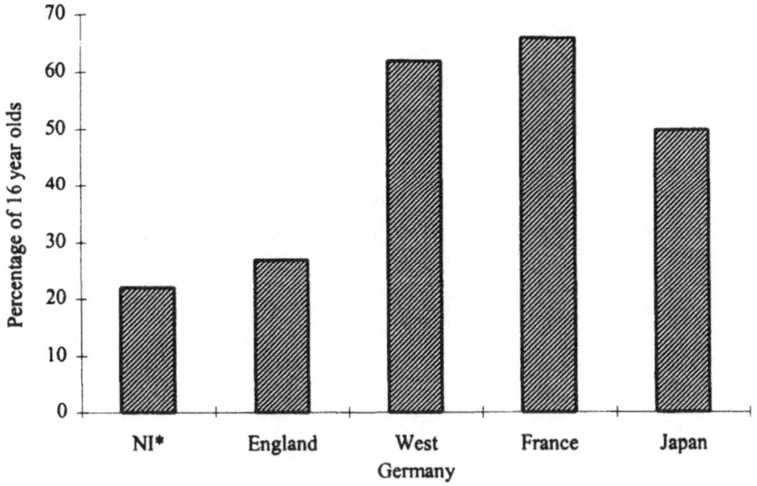

Figure 4.2 Percentage of 16 year olds reaching equivalent of GCSE grades A - C in mathematics, the national language and one science, 1990-91

* The Northern Ireland figure is based on results from the Northern Ireland Schools Examinations and Assessment Council for 1993/94. To the extent that pupils take this Council's GCSE examinations in combination with other examining boards then results for Northern Ireland will be underestimates. On the other hand, since 1993/94 is used rather than 1990/91, this may result in an upward bias because GCSE results have tended to improve through time.

Source: NIEC (1995).

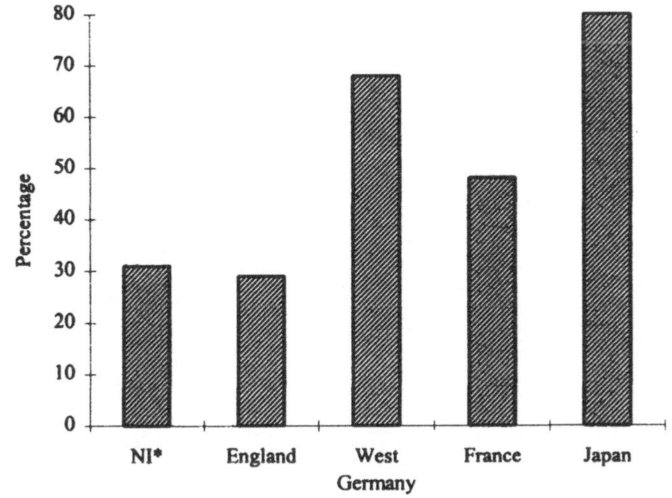

Figure 4.3 Proportion of young people obtaining two or more A levels or equivalents, 1990

* Number of school leavers with two or more passes at A level in 1990/91 and those with a National Diploma aged 17 to 19 in 1990/91 as a percentage of the mean of the 17 to 19 year old age cohorts in 1991.

Source: NIEC (1995).

5 Impact of EU Membership

Summary

An evaluation of the impact of the 1989-93 Community Support Framework suggests that by 1993 Northern Ireland GDP was 3.6 per cent higher than would have been the case in the absence of EU funding (similarly, 10,000 jobs had been created and sustained). The spending agreed under the 1994-99 Structural Fund Plan, although the annual spending figures represent an increase relative to 1989-93, is still only a small proportion of Northern Ireland GDP (less than 2 per cent). By applying a method used by the Institute of Economic Affairs (London) it is possible to estimate the net economic benefit to Northern Ireland arising from EU membership (i.e. the positive effects arising from subsidies to farm prices, free trade to the rest of the EU and the consequent incentives to greater foreign direct investment in the Province but also allowing for the negative impacts of higher food prices and taxes). This net benefit was between £260 million and £560 million in 1994 or 2-4 per cent of regional GDP. In proportional terms this net benefit was about half of that applying to the Republic of Ireland and contrasted to an estimated net cost of 1 per cent of GDP for the UK as a whole.

The impact of access to the Single European Market has the potential to effect the Northern Ireland economy in a more profound manner than the relatively small flow of financial transfers arising from Brussels. The Single Market should reduce transaction costs and hence raise profits and sales for Northern Ireland exporters. Northern Ireland's membership of the Single Market has to some degree acted as an encouragement to inward investment (though whether this was as important as other factors promoting the regional location could be disputed).

From the point of view of Northern Ireland firms the downside of the Single Market is the likelihood that competition will be increased.

The European Commission is creating pressure to 'harmonise up' regulations in regions such as Northern Ireland to the level of the more highly regulated parts of the EU. Hence, there have been changes in regulations and Directives in areas such labour market conditions and the environment.

Since Northern Ireland would currently be situated somewhere in the middle of the EU with respect to levels of rigour of regulatory standards and compliance, the pressure to harmonise is likely to raise production costs in the absence of some compensating change (e.g. with respect to technology and management) within companies. In the short run this would seem to imply a damaging effect on levels of output and employment. In the longer term, regulations could be beneficial to the extent that dynamic effects are generated though this is dependent on firms being sufficiently innovative in terms of management and technology to be able to respond to the regulatory changes so as to avoid any significant increase in costs.

Financial - The Structural Funds

This is probably the type of impact which people would most obviously think of, i.e. the inflow of funds associated with EU subsidy to local industry, agriculture or urban and community development programmes.

For the period 1989 to 1993 an overall grant support package was agreed for Northern Ireland and the other 'Objective 1' regions within the EC. This Community Support Framework (CSF) embraced the main EC structural funds, i.e. the European Regional Development Fund (ERDF), European Social Fund (ESF) and the European Agricultural Guidance and Guarantee Fund (EAGGF).

To implement the CSF Northern Ireland was given a final allocation of 702 million Ecu (£522 million). The allocation of this total between the operational programmes is shown in Table 5.1. In addition to these operational programmes there was a series of nine special community initiatives within the CSF, plus the joint INTERREG programme with the Republic of Ireland to encourage the economic development of the border counties. Whilst these initiatives were usually relatively small, they totalled £ 41 million excluding INTERREG (£57 million).

Table 5.1 Expenditure on CSF Operational Programmes, 1989 to 1993 (£ million)

	CSF Funding
Industrial development	78.4
Agricultural development	70.4
Human resources	163.3
Tourism	33.3
Transportation	123.0
Physical & social environment	38.3
Total	506.8

Source: DFP (1993), Northern Ireland Structural Funds Plan 1994-99 and Gudgin (1996). This results in a total which differs from that given in DFP (1993). The Industrial Development Operational Programme excludes £15.1 million expenditure on the natural gas pipeline on which construction began at the end of the CSF period.

Since almost all of the spending under the 1989-93 CSF had been completed by 1994 it has been possible to provide some retrospective evaluation of the effectiveness of that programme. Such evaluation could attempt to measure the gross impact of such spending e.g. the additions to company output and the numbers employed as a result. However, from the point of view of considering value for money it would be of more interest to identify their net impact. Such estimates are much more difficult to produce since they involve some allowance for the deadweight effect (i.e. how much of the investment and employment would have happened anyway given 'normal' company expansion) and the displacement effect (i.e. how far does growth in grant aided activities drive out non-assisted firms). The experience of firms in other regions may provide some indication of the extent of deadweight and displacement in Northern Ireland. The direct (e.g. employment) effects of the CSF can be identified through use of regional economic models and input-output analysis (Gudgin, 1996). These are the demand side effects. More problematic are the so-called supply side effects (because these arise from the extent to which the grant aid has made firms more competitive) which could be long lasting. NIERC estimated that the impact of the 1989-93 CSF peaked in 1993 at a cumulative boost to GDP of 3.6 per cent and of 10,000 jobs (compared to total employment of about 660,000) (Gudgin, 1996).

For the 1994-99 period the Structural Fund Plan (DFP, 1993) involved the allocation to Northern Ireland of a total of just under £1 billion. To this was added about £50 million annually during 1995-97 as part of the Peace and Reconciliation monies. In other words, the annual rate of EU assistance had increased by roughly one-half relative to the 1989-93 period. Nevertheless, in relative terms the sums of money were still relatively small; amounting to less than 2 per cent of regional GDP and only a couple of per cent of the total level of public spending (Gudgin, 1998).

Although not previously attempted, it is possible to apply to Northern Ireland a method which has already been used (Institute of Economic Affairs, London) to estimate the balance of economic costs and benefits (narrowly defined) for the UK as a whole (Table 5.2).

Positively, farmers gain by a sum equivalent to about one-half of their value added from the European subsidies to food prices. The converse of this is that every member of the Northern Ireland population has to pay higher food prices and/or higher tax to support agriculture. The net effect to the local economy is a gain of about £130 million.

Trade to the EU avoids paying tariffs, some foreign investment is attracted because of our EU membership and there are the Structural Fund payments. These are all credit items.

Narrowly defined the net economic benefit to Northern Ireland from the EU was £260-£560 million (a more sophisticated calculation would allow for: the increase in Structural Funds 1994-99, the Peace and Reconciliation money 1994-97, and the possibly negative effects of regulation and EMU; see final section of this Chapter and Chapter 6). This was a non-negligible benefit and yet still equivalent to only 2 to 4 per cent of total GDP. By comparison: total Northern Ireland GDP in 1994 was £13,216 million and total public spending about £7,500 million. The net economic benefit to the Republic of Ireland from EU membership was probably about £2,000 million (equivalent to about 6-7 per cent of GDP) and the UK as a whole probably had a net economic cost of £6,000 million (i.e. equal to about 1 per cent of UK GDP).

Table 5.2 Economic impacts of EU membership on Northern Ireland, 1994

Credit (+) or Debit (-)	Item	Amount (£ million)
+	Subsidy to prices for farmers and other, direct transfers to farming[a]	530
-	Higher food prices to consumers and higher tax payments[b]	400
+	Visible trade to EU being free of tariffs[c]	<100
+	Foreign direct investment in NI which is dependent on EU membership[d]	<200
+	Structural Funds	130

[a] Estimated using the OECD estimation of the EU average rate (as a percentage of gross output) of total subsidy to agriculture.
[b] Estimated using the OECD estimate of the EU average rate of increased food and tax bills per capita (£243).
[c] In 1994-95 Northern Ireland manufacturing exports to the rest of the EU were £1,731 million. Hindley and Howe (1996) assumed that if the UK were not a member of the EU the maximum tariff which the World Trade Organisation would allow the EU to impose on the UK would be 6 per cent. If UK firms reacted to such a 6 per cent tariff by cutting their prices by 6 per cent then total Northern Ireland manufacturing sales revenue would similarly drop by 6 per cent of £1,731 million and would produce an equivalent decline in regional income and GDP.
[d] Hindley and Howe (1996) argued that if the UK were not an EU member the deterrent impact on foreign direct investment would have an impact of no more than 1 per cent on GDP. To allow for the greater proportional importance of inward investment in Northern Ireland it was assumed that the maximum reduction in Northern Ireland GDP would have been no more than 1.5 per cent.

Sources: Using the method in Hindley and Howe (1996) and official statistics in the *NI Annual Abstract of Statistics* and *Regional Trends* (ONS).

Markets

The dynamic effect of the EU-wide market now facing Northern Ireland firms could be much larger than the effects of the Structural Funds which, as has already been shown, represent a relatively small proportion of public spending and GDP in the region. Such dynamic effects could be positive (e.g. Northern Ireland firms forced to introduce new products or adapt to more sophisticated markets and regulatory systems) or negative (e.g. because Northern Ireland firms are unable to adapt to such new challenges they simply go to the wall). The development of the Single Market since the late 1980s has decreased the transaction costs of dealing with the EU market of over 300 million potential consumers. In theory this should have increased the potential for company profits and enhance encouraged higher investment, intra-European exports and output. It should be noted that EU membership may not have been absolutely essential to gain whatever advantages follow from such a large Single Market (Hindley and Howe, 1996). After all, the alternative to the UK being a full member of the EU might be some sort of free trade arrangement in which UK firms, including those from Northern Ireland, would still be able to sell to EU without paying tariffs and in any case, under international trading rules, the ability of the EU to impose penal tariffs on the UK would have been (and would continue to be at any point in the future if the UK did decide to leave the EU) circumscribed.

Another point worth considering is that at least some of the foreign direct investment in Northern Ireland has been attracted to the Province by virtue of the UK's membership of the EU and hence the Single Market. For example, an American or South Korean firm with a plant located in Northern Ireland may be using that factory to produce goods to be sold throughout the EU Single Market. It is, however, unclear what proportion of total external investment has been induced by EU membership. There are some other very strong influences on foreign investment in the UK regions e.g. grant payments, relatively unregulated and cheap labour (see the final section of this Chapter and Chapter 4) which is English speaking.

Greater Competition

Alongside widening the markets facing Northern Ireland based firms, the Single Market also inevitably means that in such markets Northern Ireland firms will be facing stronger competition from companies in other regions/countries. Potentially this could represent a positive shock to Northern Ireland companies as they are spurred on to upgrade products and processes to meet external standards. On the other hand, the intensified competition within the Single Market might lead to the collapse of firms which were already relatively weak. It has been argued that a general effect of the Single Market will be the encouragement towards growth in average company and plant size (as firms cease to treat the EU as 15 separate national markets and begin to plan production and distribution on European-wide levels) and the regional impact of such change could be geographical centralisation of economic activity, i.e. the peripheral areas including Northern Ireland could lose employment.

Regulatory Pressures, e.g. Environmental Standards and Some of the Issues Arising from the 'Green Economy'

The economies of the EU differ in terms of their levels of regulation (both in legal standards and the extent of compliance to such requirements). Northern Ireland probably falls somewhere in the middle within the EU along with the UK as a whole and the Republic of Ireland whereas companies in, for example, Germany, Sweden and the Netherlands would face a greater burden of regulation and those in Italy and the other Mediterranean countries a lesser burden (Hitchens, Birnie, McGowan, Cottica and Triebswetter, 1998).

Two types of regulation are probably especially significant. First, regulations relating to labour including hiring and firing and health and safety since these have the effect of adding a sizeable non-wage component to total labour costs. Second, there are environmental regulations (e.g. with respect to emissions into the atmosphere and water, noise and recycling) which tend to increase production costs and may prescribe or, alternatively, proscribe certain products and processes.

The European Commission has been concerned that the existing differences between the member states represent a distortion to competition. One country could in principle use a relatively lax level of environmental or labour market regulation as a disguised instrument of industrial policy. The aim might be to encourage so-called 'social dumping' or 'eco-dumping' whereby investment moved to such a country and away from the more highly regulated economies. In fact, not all economists agree that a necessary precondition for a true Single Market is the harmonisation of social and environmental standards and legislation. Such critics of the Brussels policy would argue that it is entirely appropriate for a relatively poor country or region to choose a lower level of regulation in order to 'buy' greater economic output. In any case, the European Commission policy has tended towards the promotion of harmonised regulation and in practice this tends to mean harmonisation up to the levels of the more highly regulated economies (e.g. Germany). Both the Social Chapter and EU Environmental Directives could be seen in this light. We can then ask, if the pressure coming from Brussels is likely to increase the level of regulation on Northern Ireland firms, what is likely to be the implications of this?

The pessimistic view would stress the likelihood that in the short-term at least regulation is likely to be mainly an addition to costs. By implication both output and employment may fall. Albeit, there is every indication that environmental regulations are likely to represent only a very small proportion of total costs. The relatively unregulated state of the UK labour market may be one advantage for Northern Ireland relative to much of the rest of the EU as a location for inward investment though, as already argued, there are many other factors influencing such investment flows.

The optimistic view about regulation would stress the possible longer term benefit. Porter (1990) has pointed out that for companies which adapt to regulation at a fairly early stage there can be first mover advantages (i.e. being first in the field and establishing a temporary monopoly). Technology can also adapt to ensure that regulations can be complied with without any sizeable increase in production costs. There may even be sometimes 'free lunch' effects whereby one by-product of meeting the regulation is the company so improves its general management techniques that substantial cost savings are achieved.

Perhaps the safest conclusion to be drawn is that Northern Ireland firms will be able to meet the costs imposed by EU regulations provided their general competitiveness and productivity performance is sufficiently strong but, as the reviews in Chapters 3 and 4 have suggested, this may not be the case for manufacturing and the other tradables sectors.

6 Impact of EU Enlargement and Monetary Union

Summary

Since the 1960s Northern Ireland has relied heavily on foreign direct investment to promote industrial development. In order to attract such investment Northern Ireland had faced increasing competition from other parts of western European and, indeed, north America. The increasing levels of grants being paid to large international firms indicate how this competition has intensified. Northern Ireland has been disadvantaged by the image problem created by the Troubles. The EU enlargement in 1995 to include Sweden, Finland and Austria has further increased the competition which Northern Ireland is facing. Continued enlargement is also likely to decrease the share of Structural Funds available to Northern Ireland.

Former communist economies in eastern Europe are also now competing for foreign direct investment. Countries such as Hungary and the Czech Republic have a number of advantages which are likely to make them strong competitors to Northern Ireland. They are closer to Germany (both geographically and culturally), they have good basic apprenticeship training systems, labour costs are very low and comparative advantages have been noted in sectors such as clothing, textiles, food processing and some parts of agriculture.

The potential benefits to Northern Ireland of European Monetary Union (EMU) membership (e.g. elimination of exchange risk and the transaction costs of currency dealing) are probably quite small. On the other hand, Northern Ireland would probably lose out if the UK gave up the ability to exercise an independent monetary, exchange rate and, indeed, fiscal policy.

The development of EMU is likely to represent a wedge to further economic integration between Northern Ireland and the Republic of Ireland when the Republic of Ireland participates from January 1999 onwards but the UK exercises its opt out until at least 2002.

Competition for Foreign Direct Investment

Since the 1960s Northern Ireland has relied heavily on the attraction of foreign investment as a major instrument of regional and industrial policy. As was shown in Chapter 4 externally owned firms now represent a much larger proportion of total manufacturing industry than they do in Great Britain. Since the 1960s the total amount of potentially mobile international capital has increased several fold. However, at the same time, the demand for such projects may have grown even more rapidly as regions throughout western Europe and, more recently, the USA, offering various state assistance packages, compete to land such investments. An indication of the international competition for foreign direct investment is provided by the very high levels of grants paid (per job created) to some of the larger projects which have been attracted to various parts of Europe and north America.[1] In fact, Northern Ireland has been relatively disadvantaged given the image problem generated by the Troubles. The Scandinavian, Austrian and eastern European economies, in some cases as members of the EU of 15 countries, are now also competing for foreign direct investment and could siphon-off firms which would otherwise have come to Northern Ireland.

As the EU envisages enlargement to include 20 plus members by 2005 this will increase the demands on the regional development budget. In response to this policy dilemma the European Commission's 'Agenda 2000' document in July 1997 proposed a simplification of what are currently the six Objective Areas eligible for EU-level regional assistance down to only three categories (RSA, 1998b). The geographical coverage of the assisted areas would be cut back from 51 per cent to 35-40 per cent of the EU population through strict application of the rule that only regions with less than 75 per cent of the EU average level of GDP per capita would be eligible.

Implementation of these proposals would imply that Northern Ireland would lose its Objective One status (Northern Ireland's GDP per capita is now just above 80 per cent of the EU average). There is likely to be a transitional and gradual running down of funding (Chapter 5 discussed the scale of EU transfers to Northern Ireland).

Northern Ireland Competitive Advantages and Disadvantages Compared to the Former Communist Economies

Labour in Northern Ireland is paid much higher wages and may have not much better skills compared to some of the eastern and central European economies in such activities as basic engineering and clothing and textiles. Chapter 4 indicated that in 1995 total labour costs in Northern Ireland were at least six times higher than those in such economies as the Czech Republic and Hungary. Hitchens, Birnie, Hamar, Wagner and Zemplinerova (1995) indicated that in these countries the basic skills of operatives were good. Something like the German apprenticeship system had been preserved in these central European economies even during the communist period. Other analysts have argued that the eastern European economies with their abundant availability of cheap and relatively well-skilled labour would have comparative advantages in sectors such clothing, textiles, food processing and some parts of agriculture (Winters and Wang, 1994). Unfortunately, these are also activities on which Northern Ireland has become heavily dependent.

Pros and Cons of Single Currency Membership

There could be two principal benefits from a single currency. First, it would reduce exchange rate risk. That is, firms would no longer have to worry about exchange rate movements removing their profit margins on intra-EU trade. Supporters of the single currency have claimed that such confidence would lead to much higher trade and investment across European frontiers. Table 6.1 shows, using data from the NIERC survey of exports, that Northern Ireland exports to the rest of the EU (even excluding exports to the Republic of Ireland) already outweigh those to the rest of the world.

Critics of the single currency proposal could, however, claim that the problem of exchange risk is exaggerated. It is possible for at least the larger companies to go to the forward exchange rate market to insure themselves against short run volatility in exchange rates, or to do this in a more informal way by spreading their pattern of output sales and input purchases across various European economies.

Table 6.1 Destination of Northern Ireland manufacturing sales in 1994/95 and 1995/96 (current prices)

Destination of sales	Sales value (£ million)		Sales as a % of GDP	
	1994/95	1995/96	1994/95	1995/96
Northern Ireland	2,631	2,826	19.9	20.4
Great Britain	2,614	2,806	19.8	20.3
Republic of Ireland	631	710	4.8	5.1
Rest of EU	1,047	1,242	8.3	9.0
Rest of world	925	1,121	6.9	8.1

Source: NIERC, DED and IDB (1997).

In 1994 Northern Ireland's three largest manufacturing exporters accounted for almost one-quarter of total sectoral exports and the ten largest exporters for over two-fifths of the total. It is also worth stressing that EMU would eliminate only one type of exchange rate risk, i.e. that on trade to continental Europe. This should be good news for, say, Northern Ireland textiles and food processing companies selling to France, Italy and Germany etc. There is, however, the danger that the exchange rate between the new European currency, the Euro, and the US dollar would be more volatile than the pound sterling-dollar rate. Recent Northern Ireland export growth amongst engineering firms has been particularly rapid and it is notable that some of the largest exporters, such as Shorts-Bombardier and FG Wilson-Caterpillar, are reliant on the north American markets. There is the danger that these companies would thus suffer increased exchange rate risk. A more detailed investigation, based on export data at the level of individual firms, would be necessary to determine the balance of effects arising from tying Northern Ireland and the UK into a continental currency bloc. (Bradley and McCartan (1998) represent the first attempt to conduct such an analysis. Their results would imply that chemicals and man-made fibres would be heavily exposed to an adverse movement in the pound to Euro exchange rate whereas mechanical and electrical engineering would be highly sensitive to movements in the exchange rate between the pound and non-Euro currencies.)

The second benefit which has been claimed for the single currency is that it would eliminate the transaction costs of dealing between various currencies. In fact, such costs (e.g. commission to banks etc.) may be a fairly high proportion of the total amounts exchanged by, say, tourists but they are likely to a much smaller proportion of the larger amounts bought and sold be companies. In reality, the elimination of such costs would probably only bring a once and for all gain to EU GDP and relatively small one at that (well under one per cent).

As a region with a longstanding lag behind UK or EU best practice (this derives from a relatively weak competitiveness performance in the tradable activities, see Chapters 1 to 3) Northern Ireland should probably be more concerned about the potential costs of EMU. Two main costs can be considered. Firstly, the lost of the exchange rate adjustment mechanism and, secondly, the likelihood that fiscal policy powers will also be centralised in Brussels. As part of a single currency the UK would no longer have the ability to influence the level of the exchange rate and/or domestic interest rates according to the condition of the national macroeconomy. It is possible to envisage a situation where there would be divergence between macroeconomic conditions in, for example, Germany and the UK and as a result the UK, including Northern Ireland, would have imposed on it an inappropriate monetary policy, i.e. European wide interest rates would be either too high or too low from the point of view of the state of the UK economy. Such a possibility is made more likely given the evidence that since the mid-1980s the trade cycles in the UK and Germany have often not been synchronised When the German economy has been in boom, and therefore requiring higher interest rates to control inflation, the UK has been in depression and hence requiring lower interest rates and vice versa. The Republic of Ireland's membership of the European Monetary System (EMS) during the first half of the 1990s is illustrative of how an exchange rate and interest rate policy determined in the centre of the EU can have a damaging knock-on effect on a weaker peripheral economy. On the basis of the results of the Economic and Social Research Institute model FitzGerald (1997) concluded that German monetary policy since German unification and its consequent impact through the EMS had led to the loss of 30,000 jobs in the Republic of Ireland, mainly in the traditional activities such as textiles, clothing, food processing and basic engineering where exports were mainly directed to the UK market.

It has also been argued, for example, in the Delors Report of 1989, that one of the implications of the centralisation of monetary policy at the European level would be that fiscal policy would similarly have to lie with

Brussels. This would further reduce the ability of the UK economy to respond to a situation of, say, a relatively high rates of unemployment. It is true that fiscal policy in the UK will be constrained in any case for the rest of this decade and both the Conservative and Labour Parties have long repudiated any old style 'Keynesian' attempt to attain 'full' employment through the management of demand. At the same time, even since 1979 fiscal policy (i.e. the extent of the gap between the level of government spending and taxation which is often indicated by the Public Sector Borrowing Requirement (PSBR)) has continued to have an impact on macroeconomic performance. In technical terms, the fiscal stance, i.e. whether *if* the economy were at full employment and given the existing taxation and spending policies the PSBR would be in deficit or surplus, has varied and this did, for example, partly explain the strength of the 1983-89 boom. It is likely that EMU would rule out the possibility of adopting an expansionary fiscal stance during a slump period and might even make it difficult for a UK government to pursue a 'neutral' policy whereby the PSBR would be balanced over the trade cycle as a whole.

EMU as a Possible 'Wedge' if the Republic of Ireland Goes In and the UK Stays Out

It is looking increasingly likely (the final decision on the initial membership of the single currency 'club' was taken in the spring of 1998) that the UK will exercise its 'opt out' from initial membership of EMU in 1999. On the other hand, assuming that the whole project does go ahead, there is every indication that the Republic of Ireland will attempt to be present at the creation of the single currency. We should therefore consider the short-term and long-term effects of the Republic of Ireland being 'in' whilst Northern Ireland remains 'out' (Bew, Patterson and Teague, 1997).

In the short-term it is possible to consider two contrasting scenarios. In the first one of 'German rigour' the Euro proves to be a very strong currency. Indeed, the Germans only allow the Euro to replace the Deutschemark because they have been persuaded that the European Central Bank will follow the hard monetary policies of the Bundesbank. As the Euro appreciated against the pound this would be good for Northern Ireland exporters selling into the Republic of Ireland market and those selling to Great Britain which have Republic of Ireland competitors. A second very different scenario is one of a 'fudged EMU'. In this case, the currency can only get under way in 1999 because the Maastricht convergence criteria are interpreted in the most liberal terms.[2] The implication is that there is a lack of confidence in the new European money which sinks in value relative to the pound and US dollar. In the short run this would be bad for those Northern Ireland exporters selling either to the continental markets or competing against firms from those areas.

In the longer term is not entirely clear what the effects would be of Northern Ireland 'out' and the Republic of Ireland 'in'. There would be some retarding effect on further economic integration between the two economies but would this matter very much? Chapter 7 demonstrates that trading links across the border have not been large but they have not been smaller than the levels which could reasonably have been expected.

Notes

1. **Table 6.2 State incentive to selected international mobile projects**

Location	Year	Plant	Per employee ($)
Portugal	1991	Auto Europe, Ford VW	254,000
Alabama	1993	Mercedes-Benz	167,000
South Carolina	1994	BMW	108,000
Birmingham (UK)	1995	Jaguar	129,000
Lorraine	1995	Mercedes-Benz Swatch	57,000
South Wales	1996	LG Electronics	47,000

Source: UNCTAD statistics quoted in Economist (1997, February 1).

Quite apart from international competition there is now even subsidy competition between the UK regions. The 1992-97 the Conservative Government tried, probably unsuccessfully, to contain this. In July 1996 the LG Group, a South Korean firm, chose Wales rather than Scotland as the location for a £1.7 billion factory having been enticed by a grant package reputed to have amounted to £150 million (Economist, 1996, July 13). This level of support probably breached the limit on the amount of support per job promoted which the development agencies are meant to observe (Economist, 1996, June 8). Table 6.2 gives the cost per job figures for some recent projects.

2. At the time of writing (May 1998) this second scenario, the fudged Euro, seems more likely. This is because the European Commission's selection in May 1998 of 11 countries as eligible to join EMU (the EU15 minus the three opt-out countries of the UK, Denmark and Sweden, and with Greece excluded for the time being) involved a large amount of creative interpretation of the Maastricht criteria (the debt/GDP ratio in Belgium and Italy was about twice as high as the stated 60 per cent). Moreover, the rather peculiar circumstances surrounding the appointment of the first President of the European Central Bank (technically his term of office is eight years but he has promised to retire after four) means that the much vaunted political independence of Europe's new central bank has been compromised from the start.

7 Northern Ireland and the Republic of Ireland

Summary

Whilst some of the measured upsurge in the Republic of Ireland's economic growth rates since 1986 is genuine the official statistics exaggerate the true extent of the improvement. This is because of the extent of outflow of money to pay interest on foreign debt and also the repatriation of profits by foreign owned companies (the latter being linked to transfer pricing activities). Like Northern Ireland, the Republic of Ireland remains in most sectors a low productivity level economy.

Since the start of the 1990s there have been growing similarities between the industrial policies operated in the two Irish economies. There may be some scope for Northern Ireland to learn lessons from the Republic of Ireland.

The current extent of cross-border trade flows between Northern Ireland and the Republic of Ireland is not any less than would be expected.

The potential benefits from further economic integration between the two Irish economies, e.g. in the context of a Belfast-Dublin economic corridor, are usually relatively small.

Republic of Ireland Economic Growth 1921-88 Contrasted to 1988-97: A Celtic Tiger?

This question is considered in three sections. The first section considers whether in fact the Republic of Ireland economy has actually made the remarkable progress suggested in some of the official statistics in terms of catching up with and overtaking the UK in terms of average national income. In truth, the rumours of an emerald tiger economy have been somewhat exaggerated. The second section demonstrates that the Republic of Ireland is still a low productivity economy and, just like Northern Ireland in many sectors, lags behind the UK average or the best practice economies in the EU or elsewhere. This implies that some of the notions about great gains from Northern Ireland firms forging links with Republic of Ireland counterparts have been over-blown. The final section demonstrates that in 1994 Northern Ireland still had a considerably higher living standards level than the Republic of Ireland.

The Apparent Economic Miracle: Catching Up on the UK?

Throughout the first 65 years of independence, the 1920s until the mid-1980s, levels of GDP per capita in the Republic of Ireland were never better than two-thirds of the UK average.

Table 7.1 Gross Domestic Product[a] (GDP) per head of the population in Northern Ireland and the Republic of Ireland compared to the United Kingdom (purchasing power parity calculations, UK = 100)

	Northern Ireland	Republic of Ireland
1926	61[b]	51
1947	71	46
1960	63	47
1973	73	54
1986	79	60
1990	78	70
1991	82	77
1992	82	80
1993	82	80
1994	82	86
1995	83	91

[a] See note to Table 1.3 on GDP per capita comparisons and purchasing power parity.
[b] 1924.

Source: Johnson (1985), Kennedy, Giblin and McHugh (1988), Commission of the European Communities (1992), SOEC (1996), ONS (1997a).

This sluggish economic performance was widely noted (Ó'Gráda and O'Rourke, 1995, 1996) because the experience of other European economies would have implied that the Republic of Ireland could have been expected to narrow the gap relative to the UK. However, since 1986 apparently very rapid growth has pushed the Republic of Ireland up to over 90 per cent of the UK level, in less than one decade three-quarters of the longstanding gap in per capita national income levels has gone.

In fact the speed of Irish national income growth, and by implication the pace of convergence with the UK and the rest of the EU, has been questioned and was the subject of a Conference arranged by the Irish statistical authorities, (CSO and Irish Economic Association, 1996). The growth rates of consumption have been much more modest than those for national income (the volume of GDP at market prices grew by 30 per cent during 1988-94 but the volume of retail sales by only 18 per cent) and this has led some to suggest that much of the indicated increase in GDP is artificial and attributable to transfer pricing activities by multinationals (Murphy, 1994, 1996). It is certainly true that Gross National Product (GNP), a much more realistic measure of living standards in the Irish context since it allows for the sizeable net outflow of resources to pay interest on international debt and repatriate profits to foreign companies, has remained at least one-eighth lower than GDP throughout the period since 1986 (and in 1995 the gap may have been wider than this, GNP is indicated to have been only 86.7 per cent of GDP (CSO, 1996)).

Table 7.2 compares the Republic of Ireland's performance in terms of GNP per head of the population to other EU member states and especially some of the other areas subject to special Structural Fund assistance. The Republic of Ireland's recent record no longer appears as that of a miracle economy. During the post-Second World War period those western economies which started off with relatively low levels of income per head have generally grown more rapidly than those such as the UK, USA, Switzerland and the Scandinavian countries which were the richest countries in the 1950s. The recent performance of the Republic of Ireland falls into this pattern and has, for example, been broadly similar to that of Spain, another comparatively 'late starter' to industrialisation/economic modernisation.

If the Republic of Ireland economy had achieved substantial and real national income level convergence relative to the UK and the rest of the

EU it is likely that this would have been based on increases in productivity relative to other countries.

Table 7.2 Republic of Ireland average income per head compared to other EC members (as a percentage of the average for the pre-1995 12 members of the EC, based on purchasing power parity standards)

	1986 GDP per capita	1986 GNP per capita	1990 GDP per capita	1990 GNP per capita[a]	1995 GDP per capita	1995 GNP per capita[a]
Republic of Ireland	63	56	71	62	90	c.79
Northern Ireland	78	-	77	-	81[b]	-
United Kingdom	102	104	101	103	99	c.101
Greece	61	56	57	-	63	-
Spain	70	72	74	-	76	-
Portugal	54	51	59	-	67	-

[a] Comparative GNP per capita estimates were not readily available for 1990 or 1995, however, Republic of Ireland GNP per capita in 1990 has been estimate to have been 60 per cent of the UK level and 62 per cent of the EC12 average. The GNP per capita figures for 1995 were estimated from SOEC calculations of relative GDP per capita in purchasing power parity terms combined with the GDP/GNP ratio shown in the Republic of Ireland national accounts.
[b] 1994.

Source: As Table 7.1 and for GNP in 1986 NESC (1989), for GNP in 1990 Kennedy (1993) and SOEC (1996), Northern Ireland from PPRU (1996) as no GNP data were available at the regional level.

Still Lagging Behind the UK: A Very Low Productivity Economy

Economists measure labour productivity in order to test the capacity of various countries to generate high and rising living standards (Dertouzos,

Lester and Solow, 1989; Porter, 1990; NIEC, 1998b). It may also be an indicator of such factors as wage levels, skills, investment and attitudes to work (Hitchens, Wagner and Birnie, 1990). Table 7.3 provides some of the results of a detailed study by one of the authors of the comparative labour productivity levels in the non-service sectors of the Republic of Ireland economy since the 1930s.

Table 7.3 Republic of Ireland comparative labour productivity since the 1930s (compared using output price levels, Republic of Ireland/United Kingdom, UK = 100)

	1935	1968	1985	1990[a]	1995[a]
Manufacturing	88	82	110[b]	130	159
Agriculture[c]	61	55	77	81	85[d]
Construction	-	66[e]	91[f]	63	71[g]
Mining and quarrying	65	132	57	53[h]	59[i]
Utilities	54	47	27[j]	39[h]	29[i]
Transport	-	62[k]	-	54[l]	-
Telecommunications	-	-	-	54[m]	-
Postal services	-	-	-	62[n]	-

[a] Indices of the change in the volume of net output during 1985-90 and of the change in the level of employment were used to update the 1985 benchmark comparisons. Volume indices were then used again to update as far beyond 1990 as was possible (deflated series of total sectoral gross value added (GVA) were used for construction; SOEC, 1989a, 1994).
[b] Including an adjustment for transfer pricing (see below).
[c] Fishing and forestry were not included in these comparisons.
[d] Comparison for 1993.
[e] Using the comparative output price level of the building products industry to proxy for the comparative output price level of the building and construction sector.
[f] GVA per head using the unit value ratio for the building products industry as a proxy for construction output prices.
[g] Comparison for 1992.
[h] Comparison for 1989.
[i] Comparison for 1994.
[j] Or 45, and 58 in 1989, when gas extraction was excluded from the comparisons.

[k] Weighted average of physical productivity ratios for railways, buses and road freight.
[l] Weighted average of physical productivity ratios for railways, buses, road freight, ports, airports and airlines (a range of years, 1986-1989).
[m] Telecommunications revenues per head in 1987 compared using an appropriate purchasing power parity.
[n] Physical productivity of postal services in 1987 (items carried).

Source: Agricultural Census (UK) and Agricultural Survey (Ireland), Census of Industrial Production (Ireland) and Census of Production (UK), all for relevant years. SOEC (1988a, 1988b, 1989a, 1989b, 1994), Commission of the European Communities (1988, 1992), Department of Transport (1990), CSO (1995, 1996), Department of Finance (1995), Birnie (1996) and Cambridge Econometrics (1996).

In the mid-1980s productivity levels ranged from 27 per cent of the UK level in utilities up to 110 per cent of the level of the counterpart (in manufacturing). While Republic of Ireland productivity in construction was close to that of the sector in the UK, productivity in all the other sectors was substantially lower than that of the UK counterparts. It was not possible in every case to make comparisons for 1935 and 1968 but a number of trends could be identified.

In manufacturing and agriculture there was strong productivity convergence during 1968-85 though agricultural productivity remained substantially lower than that in the UK in 1985. There was evidence of productivity convergence in construction during the same period (admittedly it proved very difficult in construction to conduct reliable comparisons of levels and growth of productivity given variable treatment in the two national statistical sources of the smaller firms which dominate this sector). On the other hand, in mining and quarrying, utilities (i.e. gas, electricity and water) and transport the productivity shortfall relative to the UK increased during 1968-85. Where the mid-1980s results have been brought forward to later years by using the available data on the growth of the volume of output and employment the broad conclusions remain the same (the manufacturing productivity advantage relative to the UK is enhanced).

These figures indicate that the Republic of Ireland has remained a low productivity economy. Indeed, given that in many cases, at least until the 1980s, UK productivity levels were lower than those in, say, West Germany, France and the Netherlands, the Republic of Ireland shortfall compared to best practice in the EU has been even greater. The very high productivity levels implied for Republic of Ireland manufacturing since 1985 are conspicuous as an exception to this general rule. However, such levels of performance are too incredible to be explicable by other than a large measure of transfer pricing (Birnie and Hitchens, 1998). It is very unlikely to be true, as some of figures would imply that productivity levels really exceed those in the USA and Japan (usually regarded as world leaders). Rather, for accounting reasons, i.e. to take advantage of the relatively low rate of tax on profits, multinationals are attributing some value added to the Republic of Ireland which relates to activity such as R&D or marketing which occurred elsewhere in the world.

Living Standards in Northern Ireland Compared to the Republic of Ireland

The previous sections have already cast doubt on the scale of the Republic of Ireland economic miracle. Nevertheless, even if a full adjustment could be made for transfer pricing and other distortions it would remain true that the Republic of Ireland economy has grown very rapidly since 1988 and is expanding at a greater rate than at any time since independence. Levels of GNP per capita are also now at least equal to those in Northern Ireland. However, given lower rates of income taxation and higher levels of public spending, the average Northern Ireland resident still has a much higher living standard. Table 7.4 demonstrates that private consumption per head in 1994 was almost 10 per cent higher. The gap was even higher when levels of public spending were considered (this remains true even if the entire law and order budget is left out of the Northern Ireland figures). Summing together private and public spending implies that average living standards in Northern Ireland exceed those in the Republic by the order of 20 to 25 per cent.

The comparison in Table 7.4 of northern and southern living standards is open to the objection that the inclusion of all items of government spending (subject to exclusion of law and order as an extraordinary item in Northern Ireland) is too broad an approach.

For example, some items of spending might be considered as 'regrettable necessities' (i.e. they help to maintain living standards at a certain level but do not themselves add to living standards). Defence and law and order are often considered to fall within this category. Other items, e.g. welfare benefits, are transfers from government to members of the public and impact of these should already be captured by the levels of per head consumer spending. Finally, there are items of expenditure which benefit firms (e.g. much of the industrial development and training programme) as much as consumers and if there are advantages to consumers these should already have been indicated in the total consumer spending figures.

In the light of these considerations, using the Northern Ireland and Republic of Ireland public spending accounts, we selected like items of spending in both jurisdictions which were likely to have direct impacts on living standards which would not otherwise be indicated by levels of total consumer spending, i.e. mainly the spending on education, health and housing (Table 7.5).

Table 7.4 Consumption spending and public spending per head in the two Irish economies, 1994 (£ sterling)[a]

	Private consumption	Government spending	Total spending
Northern Ireland	6,236[b]	4,201[c]	10,437[e]
		4,770[d]	11,006[f]
Republic of Ireland	5,705[g]	3,063[h]	8,768[i]

[a] Republic of Ireland values converted into £ sterling using the average market exchange rate for 1994, i.e. IR£ = 0.9777£ sterling (since at the purchasing power parity rate IR£ = 0.9577£ sterling the exchange rate based comparison may slightly exaggerate the relative volume of spending in the Republic of Ireland).
[b] ONS (1996).
[c] Excluding all law and order spending, total public spending of £6,897 million divided by an estimated population of 1.6417 million.
[d] Including all law and order spending, total public spending of £7,830.7 million divided by an estimated population of 1.6417 million.
[e] Sum of Northern Ireland private consumption and Northern Ireland government spending excluding all law and order.
[f] Sum of Northern Ireland private consumption and Northern Ireland government spending including all law and order.

[g] IR£20,836 million (total consumer spending at current prices in market prices) divided by a population of 3.571 million and converted at the exchange rate. Taken from Department of Finance (1996).
[h] Budgeted expenditure of IR£11,188 million divided by a population of 3.571 million and converted at the market exchange rate. Taken from Department of Finance (1996).
[i] Sum of Republic of Ireland private consumption and Republic of Ireland government spending.

Table 7.5 Consumption spending and a narrower definition of public spending per head in the two Irish economies, 1994 (£ sterling)[a]

	Private consumption	Government spending	Total spending
Northern Ireland	6,236[b]	1,797[c]	8,033[d]
Republic of Ireland	5,705[e]	1,278[f]	6,983[g]

[a] Republic of Ireland values converted into £ sterling using the average market exchange rate for 1994, i.e. IR£ = 0.9777£ sterling (since at the purchasing power parity rate IR£ = 0.9577£ sterling the exchange rate based comparison may slightly exaggerate the relative volume of spending in the Republic of Ireland).
[b] ONS (1996).
[c] Public expenditure net (i.e. excluding EU financed spending) outturns for financial years 1993/94 and 1994/95 converted to a 1994 calendar year basis (using weights of one-third/two-thirds) and dividing by a population of 1.6417 million. The following spending Votes were included: DENI1 Education and Library Boards and further education, DENI2 higher education (in 1994/95 DENI1 combined these two areas), DHSS1 health and personal services, DOE3 water and sewerage, DOE2 housing and DOE1 road, transport and ports. HMSO (1996), NI Expenditure Plans and Priorities 1996/97 to 1998/99, London.
[d] Sum of Northern Ireland private consumption and Northern Ireland selected government spending excluding all law and order spending.
[e] IR£20,836 m (total consumer spending at current prices in market prices) divided by a population of 3.571 million and converted at the exchange rate. Taken from Department of Finance (1996).
[f] Public expenditure net (i.e. excluding EU financed spending) outturns for 1994. The following spending Votes were included: 18 transport, 25 environment (but

excluding grants in relief of rates and the fire service), 26 Office for the Minister of Education, 27 first level education, 28 secondary level education, 29 third level education, 30 marine but only harbour development, 40 social welfare but only grants for community voluntary services (exchequer funded), 41 health, 42 Gaeltachta and 43 National Gallery. Divided by a population of 3.571 million and converted at the market exchange rate. Taken from Department of Finance (1996).
[g] Sum of Republic of Ireland private consumption and selected Republic of Ireland government spending.

It is notable that when this narrower category of public spending is considered Northern Ireland's advantage increases to about 40 per cent. On the other hand, the sum of such selected government spending plus consumer spending leaves Northern Ireland with an advantage of 15 per cent relative to the Republic of Ireland. This may, however, represent an underestimate. Perhaps we have defined too narrowly those types of public spending which add to welfare over and above the measured levels of consumer spending and so a wider categorisation of comparative spending levels might still be appropriate (and this would work to Northern Ireland's advantage) and the divergence between the 1994 market exchange rate and the GDP purchasing power parity rate is suggestive that price levels, especially for consumer expenditure, may have been a couple of per cent higher in the Republic of Ireland. By implication, the volume of spending in Northern Ireland relative to the Republic of Ireland would be raised by several percentage points.

Reforms in Republic of Ireland Industrial Development Strategy post-1980: Can Northern Ireland Learn Anything?

There are a number of similarities between recent reforms in industrial policy in the two Irish economies (Bradley, 1996). In both cases, current reforms were anticipated during the 1980s (by the Pathfinder document (DED, 1987) in Northern Ireland and the Telesis Report (Telesis, 1982) in the Republic of Ireland) and the pace of change quickened from the start of the 1990s (DED, 1990, 1995; Culliton, 1992). Current policy statements in both Belfast and Dublin now give a very high place to the attainment of greater competitiveness. The hope is that if this is achieved then a higher level of employment will follow. Both sets of strategy documents contain a commitment to a more market orientated approach to industrial development together with the admission, sometimes tacit and sometimes explicit, that previous policies were often wasteful and counterproductive (see Chapter 2).

The Republic of Ireland's Culliton Report might appear to have been based on a more thorough analysis of the recent performance and problems of that country's economy (e.g. commissioned sectoral studies). The range of factors examined in Culliton and subsequently highlighted in the Dublin Government's response was broader than that emphasised in the Northern Ireland documents. For example, energy and international transport charges, the tax system and technical and vocational education. This in part reflects the difference between the Republic of Ireland as an independent state and Northern Ireland which, as a region within the UK, has less ability to determine policy in certain areas. However, even allowing for these inevitable differences, it is significant that the Northern Ireland policy documents were either written by the Department of Economic Development (DED, 1990, 1995) or agencies under its supervision (IDB, 1991, LEDU, 1991, T&EA, 1991). It remains unclear how far the policies of the other Northern Ireland Departments, Agriculture, Education and the Environment, are compatible with the DED's vision.

Both sets of documents have inspired some re-engineering of the structure of development agencies. In Dublin the Industrial Development Authority (IDA) has been split into two agencies (subject to a coordinating organisation), one with responsibility for indigenous companies and the other charged with the attraction of inward investment. Such a functional division might have some merit in Northern Ireland since some would argue it makes more sense than dividing responsibility along lines of company size (which is how LEDU and the IDB are currently defined; the former being the smaller firms of less than 50 employees and IDB taking responsibility for the rest). In Northern Ireland two new agencies have come into being: the Training and Employment Agency (T&EA) and the Industrial Research and Technology Unit (IRTU). The impact of such changes remains to be seen. There has, however, been speculation that the ongoing (in mid-1998) reviews of the agencies in Northern Ireland would recommend that Northern Ireland replicate the approach taken in Dublin with a division of responsibility by function (local/externally owned firms) as opposed to size (small/large firms).

A further similarity between the two policy changes is that both have had the good fortune to coincide with periods of improved relative economic performance. Rapid economic growth at unprecedented levels began after the mid-1980s in the Republic of Ireland and during 1990-92 Northern Ireland largely escaped the effects of the severe recession which was then effecting Great Britain (NIEC, 1993b). At the very least, these circumstances have made it easier to envisage radical changes in industrial policy (including reductions in levels of dependence on state aids) and policy makers might even claim some credit for some of the performance changes. At the same time, the upturns in relative growth performance occurred at too early a stage to be explained by shifts in policy (this conclusion is endorsed by Gorecki (1997)).

Current Extent of Cross-Border Trade and Policy Linkages: Is the Existing Level of Integration 'Too Small'?

Previous Policy Measures to Promote Co-operation

In recent years the nature and extent of economic links between Northern Ireland and the Republic of Ireland have been given great attention (Munck, 1993; Hitchens and Birnie, 1994, 1997; D'Arcy and Dickson, 1995; Bradley, 1996; Michie and Sheehan, 1998). In one sense this degree of attention has been surprising since Northern Ireland remains a UK regional economy which is highly integrated within that national economy. However, the creation of institutions to promote increased economic co-operation has been viewed in some quarters as an essential component in an overall political settlement in Northern Ireland (Bew, Patterson and Teague, 1997) and this has been official Anglo-Irish policy thinking from the Framework Document (1995) through to the 'three strand' multi-Party agreement which was eventually made in April 1998. One striking feature of the political economy of North-South co-operation in the mid to late 1990s is the number of parallels to developments about forty years previously when the then Republic of Ireland Minister for Industry and Commerce Seán Lemass declared,

> Ireland is too small a country not to be seriously handicapped in its economic development by its division into two areas separated by a customs barrier. (speech to the Oxford Union, 15 October 1959)

During 1958-65, as in the 1990s, there was a tension between the anti-partitionist rhetoric of the Dublin Government and its fear that all-Ireland arrangements might harm Southern economic interests, while the Unionist leadership, for its part, often saw the co-operation agenda as a Trojan horse for constitutional change but in practice where prepared to be pragmatic given pressure from the Northern Ireland business community (Kennedy, 1997).[1] In the contemporary debates it has been claimed that the current level of integration is less than would be reasonably expected and therefore there would be larger gains to both Irish economies through ever increasing integration. The next section considers this latter contention but first this section outlines the kinds of co-operation which were already in place by the late 1990s.

Perhaps the main area of policy intervention in order to promote cross-border economic integration has been with respect to industry and trade (Gray, 1992; Hitchens and Birnie, 1994). The Confederation of British Industry and Confederation of Irish Industry have been working jointly at a sectoral level to identify opportunities for greater trade. Chambers of Commerce in Northern Ireland and the Republic of Ireland have sponsored schemes to promote cross-border trade. Development agencies have attempted to encourage local sourcing (e.g. by the multinational plants in Northern Ireland or the Republic of Ireland) on an all Ireland basis. There has also been some pooling of research activities (e.g. by the Institute for Advanced Microelectronics which links universities in both economies).

In agriculture, fishing and forestry there have been some longstanding and successful initiatives (Matthews, 1992). For example, the common management of the Foyle Fisheries since 1952 and reciprocal fishing rights in coastal waters (this is of mutual benefit given the Northern Ireland specialism in shellfish and that of the Republic of Ireland in whitefish). Animal health programmes have also been run in parallel. Difficulties were however caused in the 1980s as divergent exchange rate movements and the consequent differences in prices to farmers provided incentives for disruptive and variable movements of animals across the border (Chapter 3). (One consequence of the 1996-98 BSE crisis was that the Republic of Ireland sealed its border to prevent the movement of cattle from Northern Ireland to further processing in the Republic of Ireland.)

There are a number of institutional links between the financial systems in the two economies (Kinsella, 1992). Once again, the breaking of the Irish pound-pound sterling parity in 1978 and the subsequent variation of the Republic of Ireland/UK exchange rate has made co-operation more difficult. This would be even more true if, as now seems almost inevitable, the Republic of Ireland attempts to be amongst the first group of members of a new European single currency but the UK decides to exercise its opt-out for at least a couple of years. Moreover, post-1979 the regulatory regime in Northern Ireland has probably moved further away from that in the Republic of Ireland. Both economies have a stock exchange but the Belfast exchange does not perform a capital raising function. Ironically, Republic of Ireland firms through their use of the one in Dublin are more integrated into the London exchange.

At the start of the 1990s 8 per cent of the Republic of Ireland's out-of-state tourist revenue derived from visitors from the Northern Ireland and the equivalent in the Northern Ireland represented 17 per cent of total tourist revenues thus cross-Border tourist flows were especially important to the Northern Ireland economy (Fitzpatrick and McEniff, 1992). There is already co-operation in terms of joint marketing and booking facilities and these were upgraded in late 1996.

In the early 1970s there was a 300 MW electricity interconnection which probably yielded a total benefit of IR£10 million annually in terms of pooling generation capacity and lowering marginal cost of supply (McGurnaghan and Scott, 1981). Repeated terrorist attack brought an end to this form of co-operation which has recently been re-instated. Pollitt (1997) notes that the main north-south interconnector was put back in place in March 1995 at a cost of £1.2 million to NIE and £0.4 million to the ESB. The savings to each system were £0.5 million annually. Pollitt (1997) reckoned that in the long run annual capacity savings would be 1 per cent of total-Ireland electricity generating costs. A number of standby links between electricity supply in the north west of Northern Ireland and the Republic of Ireland have always been maintained and the feasibility of interconnection of gas supplies in the late 1990s is being considered (Convery, 1992).

A number of formal and informal links exist in the area of transport (Crowley, 1992) such as the joint operation of the Dublin-Belfast railway. Northern Ireland firms use the ports of Rosslare and Waterford and Republic of Ireland firms Larne harbour.

There is therefore a mass of initiatives which seek to promote economic co-operation. These differ in the way in which government is involved. Some schemes are sponsored by local government, others by semi-state organisations, central government or supranational agencies (mainly the EU). In aggregate the measures are quite small relative to the total size of the economies. They tend to reflect piecemeal reaction to circumstances rather than some grand design. Measures to promote Northern Ireland-Republic of Ireland economic co-operation have thus been allowed to develop in a pragmatic and decentralised way. This may have been the most appropriate approach unless it is thought there was some alternative which would have generated larger benefits.

The next section considers the contention that the extent of cross-border trade is 'too small'. The multi-Party Stormont Castle Buildings agreement which was finally concluded on 10 April 1998 will probably not herald a quantum leap in the extent of common policy making and administrative, economic and social integration between the two Irish economies. This outcome may have been surprising given that the Framework Document (1995) had ambitious plans for cross-border executive bodies with the role of harmonising policies and economic outcomes and also with an internal 'dynamic' with respect to their range of functions. Whilst the early draft agreement from Talks Chairman Senator George Mitchell seemed to envisage very extensive powers for all-Ireland political authorities,[2] the final agreement adopted a tentative tone as to which areas of possible co-operation might be placed within the scope of the North/South Ministerial Council.[3] Up to six entirely new implementation bodies are to be created during June 1998 and June 1999 (subject to the overall constitutional package being adopted).

Do International Comparisons Suggest the Existing Level of Integration is Too Small?

Trade between the two Irish economies provides the most visible manifestation of their inter-relationship and this area has been stressed by those who claim large benefits from further linkage between the two economies (CII, 1990; Banking Ireland, 1992, September 23). In fact, as Table 7.6 illustrates, the extent of trade appears small both in absolute terms and relative to the size of the two economies. (The Table also shows that a Republic of Ireland trade surplus relative to Northern Ireland has been a longstanding feature but in neither case is the scale of exports within Ireland large relative to total GDP.)

Table 7.6 Trade between Northern Ireland and the Republic of Ireland (cross Border merchandise exports)

	From Northern Ireland		From the Republic of Ireland	
	£ million (current prices)	% of GDP	£ million (current prices)	% of GDP
1960	7.4	2.4	20.3	3.7
1972	30.9	2.9	66.9	2.9
1991	496.2	4.7	789.5	3.3
1994	537.0	4.4	722.0	2.5
1995	632.0	4.8	789.0	2.6

Source: 1960-91: Simpson (1993). 1994-95: based on a narrower definition of trade, manufacturing only, and for the financial years 1993/94 and 1994/95, Irish News (1997, March 26).

This conclusion has been reinforced by a detailed study of the export destinations of Northern Ireland manufactured products (Scott and O'Reilly, 1992). Of total sales of £6.5 billion in 1991/92 7 per cent were directed to the Republic of Ireland and in 1995/96 of £8.7 billion of sales 8 per cent went to the Republic. However, Scott and O'Reilly (1992) also cast some doubt on whether the extent of trade integration between Northern Ireland and the Republic of Ireland is actually lower than would be expected given that both are very small markets within a world or even EU perspective. For example, in proportional terms the trade flows between various Scandinavian economies were of a similar size.[4] Or, as MacEnroe and Poole (1995) noted, in 1991 Northern Ireland sold about £120 of manufactured goods to each person in the Republic of Ireland compared to Northern Ireland sales of only about £40 per head to Great Britain, i.e. at least on this measure there was already stronger trade integration between the two Irish economies than there was between Northern Ireland and the rest of the national UK market.

Evaluation of the Potential Benefit from Further North-South Co-operation

In this section we examine to what extent greater development of co-operation in general, and of the so-called Belfast-Dublin economic corridor in particular, is likely to bring benefits in terms of the expansion of four key tradable sectors, manufacturing, agriculture and food processing, tourism and producer services (there are other tradable activities but these four probably have the greatest potential for growth) (Hitchens and Birnie, 1997). In each case we seek to identify the crucial supply side or demand side constraints on sectoral growth and then consider whether the corridor is likely to have a favourable impact on such constraints.

Taking Republic of Ireland and Northern Ireland agriculture as a whole (Chapter 3) the extent of any gains from co-operation per se, whether within the corridor or beyond, are likely to be limited. This is because the main supply side constraints on performance (e.g. relatively small size of farms or lack of training of farmers; Hitchens and Birnie (1994)) are not likely to be amenable to much improvement through co-operation. There could however be some gains to co-operation between food processors within the area of the corridor in terms of improving conditions on the demand side. For example, consumer food products are likely to be aimed at urban markets and given that the corridor represents the most densely populated part of the island it would make sense for Northern Ireland and Republic of Ireland producers to treat this area as a single one for marketing purposes. The trend towards cross-border mergers, acquisitions and alliances which has begun in recent years is likely to continue and improve performance on the supply side through exploitation of greater economies of scale though it should be recognised that even all-Ireland champion firms are usually likely to remain small in wider European terms (though this is subject to the threat of monopoly and monopsony power).[5]

A sample survey study involving one of the authors (Hitchens, O'Farrell and Conway, 1996a, 1996b) indicated that producer service firms in Northern Ireland and the Republic of Ireland (which were almost entirely located in Belfast and Dublin) shared certain supply side weaknesses relative to counterparts in the South East region of the UK (e.g. absence of certain management skills or advanced items of equipment). It seems doubtful that greater development of the corridor would have much influence on such factors. Whilst mergers, partnerships and alliances between Belfast and Dublin producer service companies would have the potential to lead to the growth of larger companies in Ireland, economies of scale in most of these activities may in any case be limited. What may be crucial is the ability to achieve cost economies and favourable learning effects through specialisation in a narrowly defined activity. Given the enormous London market, sample English firms were advantaged in this respect (Hitchens, O'Farrell and Conway, 1996a, 1996b) and Dublin firms, given their local metropolitan market, relative to those in Belfast. In the context of the corridor there might be some scope for Republic of Ireland service firms to sell more in Northern Ireland by displacing purchases which had previously been made from suppliers in Great Britain. If policy makers were to promote a greater awareness of service sourcing on an all-Ireland basis this might lead to some Northern Ireland manufacturers buying in producer services for the first time (previously distance from suppliers in Great Britain had held them back from making purchases). In such circumstances not only would the Republic of Ireland suppliers gain but the Northern Ireland purchasers would probably experience improved competitiveness as the use of the services enhanced the value added of their products.

A series of supply side factors have been identified which constrain the growth of tourism. Possible uncompetitiveness in terms of price and non-price characteristics, unprofessional and poorly qualified management and congestion at popular destinations (BBC/RTE, 1992; DFP, 1993; NIEC, 1997a). The development of the corridor per se is unlikely to bring many improvements with respect to such difficulties. Admittedly, co-operation between the Northern Ireland and Republic of Ireland tourist authorities could yield returns with respect to demand side conditions e.g. joint marketing arrangements. However, given that many of the most obvious initiatives have already been applied it is not clear what more could be done. In any case, there are two major constraints which are not likely to be amenable to alteration through further development of the corridor. First, substantial growth in the number of tourists coming to Northern Ireland is unlikely in the absence of a permanent end to the Troubles and, second, the major tourist destinations in Ireland mostly lie to the west of the areas contained within the corridor (NESC, 1993b).

Development of Northern Ireland-Republic of Ireland economic links in the manufacturing sector, whether in the corridor or beyond, is unlikely to have more than a marginal effect. This is because most firms in Northern Ireland and the indigenous sector in the Republic of Ireland suffer from a syndrome of low productivity, unsophisticated products, over-emphasis on long and standardised production runs as opposed to flexible manufacturing, lagging standards in terms of human capital and cautious and out-dated management strategies. When both areas are far behind European best practice it is unclear how co-operation by itself could lead to a narrowing of the gap. Indeed, it could simply be a case of the blind leading the blind. Whilst it might appear desirable to develop external economies through co-operation within the corridor (for example, because Northern Ireland and Republic of Ireland enterprises are generally too small in comparative international terms to develop substantial internal economies of scale; Pryke (1993)) it is not going to be straightforward for policy makers to generate some sort of Marshallian industrial district or Porter cluster of firms (Chapter 2). Even without any of the frictions imposed by the border the Belfast-Dublin corridor may not be large enough, may not have a high enough density of industrial activity and may not have a sufficient range of firms to create the necessary agglomeration economies. Government policy should certainly be aimed at removing any remaining frictions impeding marketing, sourcing, company financing or partnership on an all-Ireland basis (many of these obstacles should be going anyway given the Single European Market). However, beyond this it should probably be left to the firms themselves whether they wish to carry co-operation any further.

To summarise, if the various frictions imposed as a result of the partition of the island and the corridor by the border could be shown to be key explanations of this relatively weak long run supply side performance then there might be a large gain from co-operation as a consequence of removing those frictions. However, detailed consideration on a sectoral basis suggests that in farming, business services, tourism and manufacturing most supply side weaknesses have little to do with any lack of co-operation. This is not to deny that some gains can be identified but these are not likely to be substantial. It is not co-operation per se which will be significant but initiatives to upgrade competitiveness in both Irish economies.

Estimating the Relative Scale of Benefits Arising from a Corridor

Such an estimation can be made by considering by how much Republic of Ireland and Northern Ireland output and employment would expand if competitiveness improved by comparison with the most optimistic projections of the effects increase North-South trade (this being the major and most immediate means by which co-operation would yield benefits) (Hitchens and Birnie, 1994). There is obviously no precise measure of the extent to which the Irish economies would gain if competitiveness improved, however, we proxy it by the gain to employment which would be achieved if the rate of participation in the employed labour force were to rise to the level of the UK average. This involves assuming that the relatively low current rate of participation to be largely a function of the uncompetitiveness of the tradable activities and their consequent inability to expand sufficiently to absorb more of the available labour supply though admittedly demographic factors, a young population, would also have some role. In Chapters 2 and 3 we outlined the evidence that Northern Ireland and Republic of Ireland sectoral productivity levels have remained low across most sectors and that this is a major explanation of inadequate expansion of employment in the tradable sectors. Table 7.7 gives the results.

It can be seen that the scale of benefit forecast from greater competitiveness (as proxied by variations in the level of participation in the employed labour force) far outweighs that projected from higher North-South trade. Indeed, the gains from trade on even the most favourable projection of increased trade integration would be only 16 per cent of those from increased competitiveness. Of course, not all of the 462,000 jobs arising from higher participation could be attained simply by greater competitiveness (some of the Northern Ireland and Republic of Ireland shortfall in participation is the consequence of the age structure of the population and there is also the influence of other negative factors such as the impact of the Troubles). However, even if it is assumed that only half of these 462,000 jobs could potentially be realised through greater competitiveness then such a gain would be more than three times that envisaged from greater North-South trade on the most generous assumptions (e.g. no displacement of other Irish producers and a multiplier of 2.2 such that each additional manufacturing job also generates 1.2 jobs in the service sectors).

Table 7.7 Estimation of relative scale of gains from greater competitiveness as opposed to more trade between Northern Ireland and the Republic of Ireland

	Actual employment 1992	Employment if 'more competitive' 1992[a]	Estimated gain
Northern Ireland	614,000[b]	685,000[c]	71,000
Republic of Ireland	1,125,000	1,516,000[c]	391,000
NI and ROI	1,739,000	2,201,000	462,000
Gain from greater co-operation			
A. Most favourable scenario:			
NI plus ROI with £3 billion of extra trade			75,000[d]
B. More realistic scenario:			
NI plus ROI with £0.5 billion of extra trade			7,500[e]

[a] Assuming the UK participation rate in the employed labour force applied.
[b] Assuming number of self-employed to be the same as recorded for 1991 (74,000).
[c] All participation rates were estimated using 1992 total employment figures and population Census results for 1991 (the participation rates were 39 per cent, NI; 32 per cent, ROI; and 43 per cent UK).
[d] As estimated by CBI/CII, CII (1990). Assuming a tripling of total trade volumes from 1990 levels as each Irish economy would sell as much to its neighbour, per head of the population there, as was sold at home (per capita).
[e] As estimated by Scott and O'Reilly (1992). Assuming that the total volume of trade increased by about one-half.

Source: As above and Hitchens and Birnie (1994).

The actual gains from greater trade would almost certainly be smaller. Scott and O'Reilly (1992), for example, projected total gains to manufacturing employment throughout the island of only 5,700 (the multiplier effect takes the gain to total employment to only 7,500). (They assumed that manufacturing exports in both directions would double with a

50 per cent rate of displacement of foreign products, in other words total sales of the two economies would grow by £0.5 billion). Such gains to output and employment would represent only around 0.4 per cent for Northern Ireland and the Republic of Ireland combined. In 1995/96 Northern Ireland's ratio of people in employment to people of working age was still 6 per cent lower than that of the UK as a whole. In fact, if Northern Ireland then had proportionally as many people in employment as Great Britain an extra 53,000 people would be in work (Kingon, 1998). Such a gain would far outweigh any arising from increased cross-border trade.

Policy makers should therefore consider whether any investment in developing a corridor would in fact yield greater benefit if such funds were placed into policies more directly designed to improve economic competitiveness. There are in fact a range of measures at the microeconomic level which could attempt to tackle the longstanding shortfall in terms of productivity and competitiveness and could be introduced alongside the 'shock' provided by the downgrading of traditional industrial policy and the high rates of general subsidy which often accompanied such policies. Such a new direction for policy would be consistent with the current commitment by the authorities to move towards a more selective and 'software' orientated grant regime; DED (1990), Culliton (1992), Government of Ireland (1993), DFP(1993) and see also Chapter 8. There should be more recognition that the shortfall in productivity and competitiveness is probably caused partly by relatively low levels of product quality as well as by relatively low levels of physical productivity (Hitchens, Wagner and Birnie, 1992; Roper and Hoffman, 1993; Roper, 1997). Issues of physical productivity such as scale, capital intensity and industrial relations have traditionally been emphasised by economists and governments. However, much less is known as to how and why economies differ in terms of the range of products produced, their qualities, markets served and future prospects (Porter, 1990). Questions of product quality lead on to investigations of management training and experience and company strategy. Policy intervention in the future should be directed towards promoting higher value added products and this would imply that policy makers will require much better information about the relative quality of management in Northern Ireland and the Republic of Ireland (one possible research methodology to untangle why strategies and quality differ would be through managerial exchanges between matched firms (Hitchens, Wagner and Birnie, 1991; Hitchens and Birnie, 1993, 1994)).

Our scepticism about the prospects for a corridor is one reflection of a wider disillusionment as to the potential for so-called 'super regions' within western Europe. At one time it was envisaged that the EU Single Market would facilitate the creation of huge transnational economic regions. The Atlantic Arc including the island of Ireland, the 'Celtic fringe' of Great Britain and the coast of 'mainland' Europe from Brittany to Portugal was to be one of these. More sober reflection has suggested that there are limits to the extent to which increased integration between these economies can be envisaged (Gripaios and Gripaios, 1992). Moreover, it may be over-optimistic to suppose the Atlantic Arc can imitate the apparent success of the Pacific Rim economies. The priority for all the Atlantic Arc economies including Northern Ireland, and this is especially so since the Single Market is likely to increase competitiveness and centralising pressures within western Europe, is probably to intensify and improve their transport, logistical, technological, human capital and other links with the relatively more successful core regions of the EU.

Notes

1. By 1958 there was co-operative management or administration of schemes such as the Foyle Fisheries, Erne hydro electric, cross-border electricity links and the Belfast-Dublin railway line.
2. The proposed all-Ireland political authorities were to be free standing in the sense that they were not in any way accountable to a Northern Ireland Assembly and would derive their legislative authority and, presumably funding arrangements, from Dublin and London. Paragraph seven of the Strand Two (i.e. Northern Ireland-Republic of Ireland relationships) proposals of the original Mitchell draft said

> For the areas listed in annex C, where it is agreed that the new implementation bodies are to be established, the two governments are to make all necessary legislative and other preparations to ensure the establishment of these bodies at the inception of the agreement... such that these bodies function effectively as rapidly as possible" (Trimble, 1998).

The Unionist fear was that once such bodies came into being a united Ireland government would inevitably grow from the embryo.

Annex C (of the Mitchell draft) listed eight bodies: Annexes A and B also listed respectively 25 and 16 other areas for immediate cross-border co-operation. Some of these were modest, but others included the harmonisation of further and higher education and general hospital services, as well as the creation of all-Ireland bodies to run trade and the arts (Trimble, 1998).

3. The 10 April agreement listed the following 12 areas as ones were co-operation through the North/South Ministerial Council might be possible:

1. Agriculture - animal and plant health;
2. Education - teacher qualifications and exchanges;
3. Transport - strategic transport planning;
4. Environment - environmental protection, pollution, water quality and waste management;
5. Waterways - inland waterways;
6. Social security/social welfare - entitlements of cross-border workers and fraud control;
7. Tourism - promotion, marketing, research and product development;
8. Relevant EU Programmes such as SPPR, INTERREG, Leader II and their successors;
9. Inland fisheries;
10. Aquaculture and marine matters;
11. Health - accident and emergency services and other related cross-border issues;
12. Urban and rural development.

4. A similar point can be made by drawing a comparison with trade flows within the Iberian peninsula. In 1986 Spanish exports to Portugal were 2.2 per cent of its total and in 1997 still only 5.4 per cent (Economist, 1998, February 14) and Portugal's population is about three times that of the Republic of Ireland and six times that of Northern Ireland.
5. There might be gains to inter-firm co-operation in food processing and especially in dairying where both Irish economies may have a natural resource-based comparative advantage and hence some competitive edges (see Boyle, Kearney, McCarthy and Keane (1991) for a relatively optimistic view of the Republic of Ireland's prospects in this sector and Hitchens and Birnie (1993) and Davis (1991) for more gloomy views regarding this industry in Northern Ireland and the Republic of Ireland). As Table 2.6 illustrated at least one of the Republic of Ireland based dairying groups, Kerry, is already relatively large by European standards.

8 Policies, Peace and Prospects

Summary

The first section of this Chapter summarises industrial development strategy in Northern Ireland from 1945 until the late 1980s through considering the experience of the use of the various instruments of regional policy such as labour and capital subsidies, inward investment, training and science and technology policies. Some discussion of developments in the Republic of Ireland is provided as a comparison.

The shift in Northern Ireland industrial policy in 1990 towards a much greater emphasis on the attainment of competitiveness is then described. The Department of Economic Development emphasis on competitiveness points in the right direction. However, it is still too early to judge whether the change in policy from 1990 onwards has produced improvements in economic performance.

Finally, the prospects for the economy with special reference to the impact of political developments and an agenda of policy issues are evaluated.

Industrial Development Policy in Northern Ireland 1945-90

Introduction

Industrial policy in Northern Ireland before 1990 could be appraised in terms of the record of five different instruments of policy:

- Labour subsidies;
- Capital subsidies;
- Inward investment;
- Training and educational policy;
- Science and technology policy.

Labour Subsidies

How do these work? By lowering the cost to the employer of taking on additional workers and so, at least in theory, reducing the price of labour relative to that of capital. This should encourage an increase in labour demand and hence a reduction in unemployment (in microeconomic terms some positive substitution effect in favour of the use of labour, and away from capital, in response to this shift in relative prices would be expected).

Positive points relating to this instrument It represents a direct subsidisation of the factor of production which is usually in over-supply in the depressed region, i.e. labour (Armstrong and Taylor, 1993). Thus, in theory at least, it offers the prospect of achieving socially desirable goals without generating a host of price distortions and hence allocative inefficiencies across a range of markets (alternative policy interventions to attempt to deal with unemployment might involve, for example, altering the exchange rate or interest rate and these could have wider impacts on efficiency).

Negative points relating to this instrument Labour costs are usually only a small proportion of total costs and in some parts of manufacturing (i.e. the more capital intensive sectors such as in engineering or chemicals) would be very low in proportional terms. Given this, a reduction of X per cent in labour costs will, at best, lead to a reduction in total cost of some value much less than X. There is, in any case, no guarantee that any cost reduction would be passed on in the form of lower product prices (though it would if firms were using a mark-up pricing procedure). Even if sales were to increase productivity rather than employment might go up (though, from the point of view of regional incomes, company competitiveness and long-term survivability this would not necessarily be an undesirable outcome). In some cases, the labour subsidy might simply be treated as a compensating factor for low profitability in certain firms. There is some evidence that this did happen in Great Britain.

Experience of labour subsidies in Northern Ireland Northern Ireland, like the rest of the UK, operated the Regional Employment Premium (REP) between 1968 and 1978 (1977 in Great Britain). This was a flat rate subsidy for each employee in manufacturing in the Special Development

Areas (i.e. central Scotland, south Wales, north east and north west England) plus Northern Ireland which was equivalent to about 7 per cent of the average male manufacturing wage in Northern Ireland but only 2 per cent of total costs (these proportional effects were slightly stronger in Northern Ireland than in the rest of the UK given that wages levels were on average about 20 per cent lower, see Chapter 4). Survey evidence suggested that across the UK only about one-half of the firms which benefitted from the REP cut their sales prices. For Northern Ireland, Roper and O'Shea (1991) estimated a small positive employment effect by early 1980s (about 3,000 jobs) but at a high cost, £570 million. By implication, this represented a very high cost per job created. Similarly, the shift-share analysis of Moore, Rhodes and Tyler (1987) implied the cost per job created by the REP, and sustained through to 1981, was of the order of £73,000 in 1981 prices (compared to the then average manufacturing wage of only £6,000). This was about three times the cost per job estimate for capital grants and cast great doubt on the cost effectiveness of the instrument.

Conclusion on labour subsidies in Northern Ireland Labour subsidies have moved out of favour. Increased employment is now seen as the outcome of other policy objectives (mainly of greater competitiveness). However, there is still use of something like labour subsidies when these are targeted on types of unemployed, e.g. the long-term or youth unemployed (for example the Welfare to Work and New Deal programmes initiated by the incoming Labour government in 1997-98).

Capital Subsidies or Grants

How do they work? These lower the net cost of capital to the firm. The lowering of the cost of capital relative to labour is, other things being equal, likely to raise the capital-labour ratio (i.e. the substitution effect taken by itself would cut employment). This, of itself, might lower the number of jobs but if there is also the generation of increased competitiveness and profits and so, there could perhaps be higher output, and hence, in turn, higher employment (in theory, there could be a positive income effect).

Positive points relating to this instrument It is likely to increase investment and the size of the capital stock and by implication modernise industry (perhaps making it more competitive in interregional and international terms).

Negative points relating to this instrument It is theoretically possible that employment could drop as a result of this instrument (this would usually be considered a perverse outcome when policy is designed to aid a high unemployment region). It is in fact more likely that employment creation would still take place but that it would be expensive (especially in the capital intensive industries). Analysis of regional policy in Great Britain during the 1970s suggested that in some sectors (such as oil refining) regional policy spending was associated with costs per job of several £100,000 per job created and sustained until 1981 (this was at a time when the average annual manufacturing wage was only about £6,000). There is the possibility of deadweight (grant assistance given to investment which would have happened anyway). This is less likely when firms are sure they will succeed in getting a grant payment and therefore take this into account in their investment appraisal methods. There may be displacement, i.e. assisted firms grow at the expense of non-assisted ones within the same region such that there is little or no net benefit. A further worrying possibility is that of inappropriate purchases (i.e. because of the reduced net cost to them firms buy too much machinery or machinery which is in some sense too sophisticated relative to their needs or capabilities).

The experience of capital grants in Northern Ireland From the early 1950s through to the late 1980s capital was very heavily subsidised in Northern Ireland (see also Chapter 2). The employment generation which did occur was expensive though almost certainly to a lesser degree than the REP. There was evidence of deadweight (indeed, the relevant Northern Ireland civil service department, the Department of Economic Development, claimed this as the main reason for phasing out capital grants from 1988 onwards). There was also, particularly in matched plant comparisons with firms in other British Isles or European regions, evidence of inappropriate machine purchases (Hitchens, Wagner and Birnie, 1990).

Conclusion on capital grants During the 1950s-80s capital grants were the main instrument of regional policy in Northern Ireland as in the rest of the UK. The bulk of the jobs arising from policy efforts could be attributed to capital grants. By the end of the 1980s, however, there was disillusionment with capital grants. They were perceived as expensive and sometimes counterproductive. Capital grants were officially phased out after 1988 though one irony of current industrial policy in Northern Ireland is that, notwithstanding the attempts to reform policy after 1990, most grant aid to industry is still being spent on capital assets (Gorecki, 1997). This anomalous situation may have been reinforced by the decision of the Chancellor of the Exchequer on 12 May 1998 to grant 100 per cent first year capital allowances for all small and medium sized enterprises in Northern Ireland (see below).

Inward Investment

How does this instrument work? Northern Ireland has shared in the 'carrot and stick' approach to inward investment which has been adopted in the UK during most of the period since the Second World War. On the one hand, until 1981 regulations were in place which attempted to limit industrial expansion in what were then deemed the 'congested districts' of the country (i.e. mainly the South East region of the UK) with the intention of forcing companies to expand in the northern and western regions of the UK. On the other hand, a range of grants, such as the labour and capital subsidies discussed previously, were intended to provide incentives to draw firms into the depressed regions. In contrast to the Republic of Ireland, Northern Ireland did not use variations in the rate of corporate profit taxation as a carrot to inward investors.

Positive points It offers the opportunity for quick increases in investment, output and employment. Direct investment also makes it possible to bring in outside technology as well as management techniques and access to wider marketing networks

Negative points In practice this instrument has proved expensive in terms of the cost of jobs created and this has been increasingly so over time (given competition from regions in western Europe and, now, eastern Europe too, as well as the USA and east Asia). In general, inward investment has not proved to be a means to pull in high technology projects. In fact, the plants which have been established have often been vulnerable to withdrawals from peripheral regions by the multinationals. Rates of linkage to suppliers have proven to be low.

Experience of inward investment in Northern Ireland In Northern Ireland too, this instrument has proven expensive and increasingly so in the 1970s and 1980s (especially in terms of jobs created as opposed to promoted). A relatively high rate of closures in the region (Fothergill and Guy, 1990) prompts the question whether one impact of the Troubles was that the portfolio of inward investment projects attracted into the region was unusually risky. The duration of the jobs created has been low on average and rates of spending on R&D have typically been low (Harris, 1991). Rates of local sourcing have also been low.

Conclusion with regard to inward investment There has been some disillusionment with the use of inward investment but there is still the official perception this is a game Northern Ireland cannot afford to leave even if the cost in terms of grant payments is high. Such a perception was written into the 1990 and 1995 policy documents (DED, 1990, 1995).

Training and Education

How does this instrument work? Through raising the quantity of human capital in the regional economy which, according to both the neoclassical and endogenous theories of economic growth (see Chapter 1), should lead to at least higher levels of output per worker and perhaps even a cumulative process of economic growth. Some commentators have noted that regions with favourable endowments of human capital are more likely to attract high quality foreign direct investment (i.e. multinational branch plants which include locally based R&D functions and other higher order management activities) (Reich, 1990). A further benefit is that increased training should to some extent increase the efficiency of the labour market and hence reduce frictional and structural unemployment.

Positive points This approach of relying heavily on the upgrading of the stock of human capital has been adopted in the UK, USA and many other countries. Training and education has certain external benefits to the extent that it probably raises productivity levels and growth prospects across the economy (Prais, 1981; Hitchens, Daly and Wagner, 1985) and it also increases the likelihood that those who have been trained will be employed and will earn relatively high wages. Education and training policy thus has the potential to attain objectives of both economic efficiency and social equity (NESC, 1993c; NIEC, 1997d).

Negative points During the 1970s and 1980s it became commonplace to emphasise the weakness of technical and vocational education as a major explanation and perhaps the key reason for the UK's relatively weak performance in manufacturing. This was in fact not a new argument and had first appeared in the mid-nineteenth century (Hitchens, Wagner and Birnie, 1990). This then begs the question as to at which level training and education policy should start. Should it, for example, prioritise nursery schooling, primary or secondary level basic literacy or numeracy, craft-type skills, technical level qualifications, degree level engineering qualifications, in-company training, third level management skills and so on? (NIEC, 1997d.) A number of international studies have suggested that, whereas the UK has traditionally devoted relatively generous public funding to tertiary level education and less so to the secondary and primary levels, the social returns might be greatest for the education of the younger age groups and perhaps especially for nursery education. A second problem is that education and training policy usually entails a heavy cost both in terms of the direct spending required and also with respect to opportunity costs (e.g. the opportunities for paid employment foregone by those participating in a period of education). The question therefore arises who should pay for such policies - the government, the individuals being trained or the employers or some combination of these? Microeconomic theory implies a case for some public subsidy given that education and training usually does generate some positive externalities but the private returns to education suggest that the individuals should also pay for some of the cost.

Experience of education and training in Northern Ireland During the 1960s-80s Northern Ireland largely followed the UK training approach (i.e. most school leavers, at 15-16, proceeded to be trained on the job and a relatively small number of these, by Continental standards, undertook apprenticeship training to craft level and some of this more rigorous training was encouraged by policy through a mixture of subsidy and levies on firms). From the 1980s onwards there was shift towards publicly financed schemes to contain unemployment and particularly youth unemployment (though the extent of training in such projects was usually low). In the 1990s Northern Ireland has shared in a UK-wide concentration on human capital to raise competitiveness. The application to the region of the 1980s educational reforms has helped to reduce the number of school leavers without formal qualifications (NIEC, 1997d) though there has to be a suspicion that quality standards have been diluted. To an even greater extent than Great Britain there has been increased participation at the tertiary level such that by the late 1990s over one-third of the 18-21 age group were going to university. However, a high proportion of these (about 40 per cent) were leaving Northern Ireland to study elsewhere and the rate of return of these graduates has been low. Thus Northern Ireland's potential stock of human capital has been reduced by its own version of the brain drain (probably another negative effect produced by the Troubles).

Science and Technology Policy

How does this instrument work? Once again, as with educational and training policy, the theoretical basis of this is a particular view of the causes of economic growth. In endogenous growth theory (see Chapter 1 and Hitchens and Birnie (1994)) spending on R&D is an input to the growth process and one characterised by increasing returns (i.e. an expansion in R&D of X per cent could lead to growth in GDP of more than X per cent). Moreover, a thriving domestic R&D sector is more likely to attract into the region/country multinational branch plants which have sophisticated technological activities attached. The microeconomic argument for some degree of governmental subsidy of scientific and technical activities is that some of the returns to these are positive externalities, i.e. they cannot be entirely appropriated by the individual firm which invests in the R&D and so there is the danger of market failure whereby private companies would choose a level of R&D spending which was less than that which was socially desirable.

Positive points Other countries have adopted this approach and in fact pretty much every developed economy now has some form of public support for science, technology and innovation activities (Dunford and Hudson, 1996; NIEC, 1998b). A successful outcome to such policies would contribute to potential for wealth creation

Negative points Notwithstanding hype about 'silicon valleys, glens and fens' (e.g. central California, central Scotland and Cambridge-East Anglia), in most cases the numbers of jobs generated through clusters of so-called high technology firms is fairly small. What is certainly true is that a region/country cannot simply wish a high technology sector into existence. Where such networks of firms have prospered this has usually been because of a supply appropriate factors of production (e.g. graduates from local universities) and/or a history of success in a linked industrial sector (Porter, 1990).

The experience of science and technology policy in Northern Ireland During the 1960s-80s in Northern Ireland, as in other assisted regions of the UK, R&D grants were on offer but the rate of take-up was disappointingly low. At the beginning of the 1990s the average rate of R&D spending in Northern Ireland manufacturing was far behind the UK average (itself not a leader in western European or developed economy terms) and apart from a few large manufacturing companies and publicly financed activity by the Department of Agriculture Northern Ireland there was almost no R&D going on anywhere within the region (NIEC, 1993a).

Most commentators have reckoned that the extent of external ownership and small average size of firms/plants are powerful explanations of this situation (Harris, 1991). On the basis of international comparisons of managerial attitudes and competencies, Hitchens, Wagner and Birnie (1991) argued that company strategy was also a large part of the explanation. Northern Ireland companies simply did not want to take the risk of engaging in product strategies dependent on taking risks with respect to product innovation (this complacency is understandable because hitherto they have been able to earn reasonable profits through making standardised products and traditional industrial policy with its heavy rates of subsidisation of capital could have reinforced this situation). The reforms of industrial policy initiated since 1990 were intended to give more impetus to scientific activity though it is unclear whether much improvement had been wrought by 1998.

On the more positive side, the two universities in Northern Ireland now produce a considerable number of graduates in computer science and other information skills activities and it appears this may be giving the region something of a competitive edge in what is potentially an important tradable service.

Policy Changes in Northern Ireland in the 1990s

The immediate context for the evaluation of the post-1990 competitiveness strategy in Northern Ireland appears very favourable given that recent Northern Ireland manufacturing output growth has outstripped that of the counterpart sector in Great Britain. During 1991-95 the volume of manufacturing output grew by 15.5 per cent compared to the UK average of 5.1 per cent (during 1989-96 as a whole the manufacturing output growth in Northern Ireland was 18 per cent compared to a UK average of 6.7 per cent, Gorecki (1997)). The increase in numbers of employees in employment was also impressive. Fourteen per cent in Northern Ireland during 1987-96 compared to only 3 per cent in the UK.

It has been debated whether this could be attributed more to demand side factors (i.e. the weak development of the 1983-89 house price and credit boom in Northern Ireland alongside the continued size of the public sector shielded Northern Ireland from the 1990-92 national economic downturn, Gudgin (1991), NIEC (1993b)) or some sort of supply side renaissance, though one perhaps partly attributable to the relatively high rates of industrial development spending in the Province, with Northern Ireland at last making up a longstanding competitiveness shortfall relative to the rest of the UK? If the latter, as has been implied by Gudgin (1995), then some narrowing of the chronic manufacturing productivity gap might be expected.

The improvement in Northern Ireland's manufacturing comparative growth performance has been accompanied by changes in industrial policy. The 1990 DED document (DED, 1990) which laid the basis for the reshaping of policy contained two key emphasises. Firstly, it said that government assistance to industry should become more selective. In future grant and other support should be conditional on firms showing improvements in their competitiveness performances. Secondly, such support should also be more restricted in its scope. The government should only step in where markets had failed. Unfortunately, neither this document nor the follow-up ones produced by the agencies (IDB, 1991, LEDU, 1991, TEA, 1991) stated clearly how the concepts of 'competitiveness' and 'market failure' were going to be operationalised (Hitchens and Birnie, 1991; Hitchens, Wagner and Birnie, 1992; NIEC, 1994b).

Subsequently, the official line was that the policy was one of 'backing winners', i.e. firms which according to indicators such as profitability, growth or market shares were demonstrably competitive would then receive further governmental support. The 1990s reforms can be seen as a reaction against the policies of the 1960s and 1970s which were perceived as having certain counter-productive effects (Harris, 1991; Hitchens, Wagner and Birnie, 1990; Borooah and Lee, 1991). For example, high rates of grant support to capital had been associated with high investment rates and also low utilisation of machinery, together with waste and low levels of capital productivity without any significant gains in comparative labour productivity (see Chapters 2 and 3). Alongside the change in official policy, the private sector in Northern Ireland has attempted to adopt a co-operative and pro-active approach to industrial development, the Northern Ireland Growth Challenge (NIGC, 1994). Whilst broadly accepting the lines of the governmental strategy (e.g. the focus on competitiveness and selective assistance) the NIGC has added the emphasis that if ambitious growth targets are to be realised (e.g. 60,000 net job creations by 2000 and convergence to the UK average GDP per capita level by 2005 compared to only four-fifths of that level in 1995) then the development of competitive industrial firms in clusters (i.e. firms interlinked by linkages and external economies) will be necessary.

Evaluation of the 1990s Competitiveness Strategy

As was demonstrated in Chapter 2 with respect to manufacturing productivity, during 1980-92 there was not much change in the pattern previously established between 1912 and the 1980s. We also indicated that it is unlikely that either the capital stock or the structural effect were the main explanations for the continuing productivity gap. It is likely that the same factors which were previously identified still apply i.e. management, skills and flexibility of the labour force, R&D and innovation and product quality and market positioning, and the restricted scope for agglomeration economies given the small size and undiversified scope of the Northern Ireland manufacturing base. Interestingly, these were the sorts of factors which were indicated as likely to be important when Northern Ireland was compared with more successful regions in western Europe (Dunford and Hudson, 1996). Roper (1995) additionally implied that relatively small size of plants could be a key explanation of the Northern Ireland productivity shortfall. Chapter 3 reinforced this depressing story by indicating the relatively weak competitiveness performance of Northern Ireland in a range of sectors other than manufacturing such as agriculture, business services and tourism.

In the light of all of this the DED (1990, 1995) strategy probably points in the right direction but it is still too early to tell whether the reforms in the systems of industrial support are yielding any acceleration in productivity growth (at the time of writing, the 1990s competitiveness strategy is itself the subject of an official review and alongside this Northern Ireland's 'Treasury', the Department of Finance and Personnel, is conducting a comprehensive review of spending). Unfortunately, the stability of the manufacturing productivity gap during 1912-92 (Chapter 2) does not suggest grounds for optimism that sudden improvements can be expected.

At least some of the differential boost to the Northern Ireland economy came from the public sector. Table 8.1 illustrates the development of public spending in Northern Ireland during the 1990s and indicates how the level remained considerably greater than in Great Britain in proportional terms. In fact, during 1992/93 to 1994/95 the real level of public spending grew by 7.3 per cent compared to an average growth for the UK of only 2.2 per cent. And, as was noted in Chapter 2, Northern Ireland is unlikely to enjoy a similar growth in public spending in the immediate future. Table 8.2 confirms the relatively heavy dependence on the public sector in Northern Ireland by comparing the size of public and private sector employment.

Admittedly, manufactured sales outside of the region have grown which might indicate some improvement in competitiveness and hence growth which is private sector-led. However, Gorecki (1997) stresses that Scotland and Wales similarly enjoyed expansions in manufacturing output during the early 1990s which were several times the UK average. He suggests that the critical factor was the high level of aggregate demand in the economy as a whole and in the South East in particular. As the regional economy in the South East reached full capacity then firms in the outer regions got opportunities for higher sales. To the extent that this is true then the relatively rapid growth experienced in Northern Ireland at that time was partly a cyclical phenomenon (the optimist might reply that once Northern Ireland firms have broken into the market in the South East they will continue to expand their market share, this remains to be seen).

Table 8.1 Spending by the Northern Ireland Civil Service Departments[a] in the 1990s

	Total spending (£m)	% of NI GDP	Government spending as % of GDP in comparison areas		
			UK	ROI	Average Western economies[b]
1990/91	5,525	54	39.9	41.2	46.1
1991/92	6,018	54	-	-	-
1992/93	6,580	56	-	-	-
1993/94	7,085	57	-	-	-
1994/95	7,407	56	-	-	-
1995/96	7,823	56	-	-	-
1996/97	8,015	-	41.9	37.6	47.1
1997/98	8,210	-	-	-	-
1998/99	8,273	-	-	-	-

[a] Excluding some public spending by UK Departments which falls within Northern Ireland. There were also small upwards revisions to spending in Northern Ireland as a result of the first two Budgets of the Labour Government elected in 1997 (NIEC, 1997b) and the apparently successful conclusion of the multi-Party political negotiations led to the Chancellor of the Exchequer producing a special package of additional spending for Northern Ireland on 12 May 1998 (£215 million over four years).

[b] Average of Austria, Belgium, Canada, France, Germany, Italy, Japan, Netherlands, Norway, Spain, Sweden, Switzerland, UK and USA.

Source: Economist (1997, September 20); Northern Ireland Statistics and Research Agency (1997).

Table 8.2 Public sector employment as a percentage of total private sector employment, Northern Ireland, United Kingdom and the Republic of Ireland, 1970 to 1995

	1970	1985	1995
Northern Ireland	26.3[a]	41.4	39.4[b]
United Kingdom	22.2	27.4	16.8
Republic of Ireland	13.1	21.8	22.4

[a] 1971.
[b] 1993.

Source: NIEC (1998c).

Gorecki (1997) notes, as we have done in Chapters 2 and 3, there are few indications that sectoral comparative productivity has improved much since the start of the 1990s strategy. Improvements in comparative cost competitiveness have been bought at the price of accepting a downward drift in wage levels relative to the rest of the UK. This is an approach to competitiveness which is neither desirable nor, in the long run, likely to be sustainable (the national minimum wage will act as a floor below which Northern Ireland wages cannot fall). He further notes (see also Chapter 2) that there is little evidence of a reduction in the levels of spending on industrial development. Nor in practice, and notwithstanding the official phasing out of the capital grant, has there been a shift in the allocation of the budget away from the subsidy of hardware, e.g. machines and factories, towards 'software', i.e. management skills, training, consultancy and R&D. With respect to the current vogue for trying to apply Porter's notion of networked based business development, it is significant that during this 80 year period the type of clustered industrial development which the NIGC now envisages as so important failed to appear.

One major uncertainty hanging over industrial policy in Northern Ireland is the political situation in Northern Ireland. Firstly, how likely is a political settlement and would this lead to permanent peace? Secondly, even if peace is attained what would be the scale of net impacts on the local economy? The latter question is considered in the following section.

Prospects for the Northern Ireland Economy

There are three parts to this consideration. In the first we use a series of rough procedures to estimate the scale of economc costs of the Troubles during 1969-97. In the second we weigh up the positive and negative demand side and employment effects of a substantial decrease in paramilitary activity and the achievement of political stability. Finally, in the third section, we review some of the outstanding questions relating to the prospects for the economy.

The Economic Cost of the Troubles, 1969-97

Quite apart from the hideous loss of human life[1], it is possible to place a rough economic cost on the Troubles in Northern Ireland under three headings - personal injuries, material damage to the economy and increased law and order spending.

Personal injuries Since 1969 about 31,500 people resident in Northern Ireland have been injured. (Some sources suggest an even higher figure and in addition, about 5,300 members of the Regular Army, mainly from Great Britain, have been injured.) A monetary value on such injuries could have two components:

- A certain number of those 31,500 people will have lost an amount of working years as a result of their injuries. We could therefore consider the cash cost in terms of earnings foregone;
- For those who lose some working time and also for those who would not be working in any case (the young, the old and the unemployed) some other sum of cash could be imputed, probably somewhat arbitrarily, as equivalent to the distress created by the injuries.

In the absence of detailed information on those injured and on their subsequent work histories one could make the conservative assumption that the average equivalent cash cost of each injury was equal to one-tenth of the sum used to represent the value of a human life, i.e. £ 70,000[2]. This would give a total of £2.2 billion (i.e. 31,500 times £70,000).

Material damage to the economy One could add-up the costs of property damaged and destroyed, the foreign direct investment which was deterred, local investment which was discouraged and tourists who did not visit the Province. In practice data at that level of detail does not exist. Moreover, the total value of discouraged investment and tourist business can only be imputed by use of some counterfactual, i.e. how would the Northern Ireland economy have developed after 1969 in the absence of political violence and instability. As above we have therefore opted for a rough procedure which might well underestimate the impact of the Troubles. If, say, the impact of all the material damage was to reduce the annual growth rate of the economy by 0.5 per cent then the average annual cash cost would have been around £50 million in 1997 prices. This would produce a total figure of £1.4 billion (i.e. 28 times £50 million).

Higher law and order spending than would otherwise have been necessary The late 1990s law and order spending within the Northern Ireland Budget was about £1 billion. If we assume that in the absence of the Troubles that level of spending could be as low as £500 million then this represents an annual Troubles 'cost' of £500 million (comparison with levels of policing in Northern Ireland pre-1969 or other regions of the UK at the current time might even imply deeper cuts in the security budget in the absence of political violence, Bew, Patterson and Teague (1997)). Given that the level of public spending on law and order has increased over time in real (i.e. inflation adjusted terms) we take the 1980 annual spend of about £600 million (in 1997 prices) as the annual average for the whole of the 1969-97 period and assumed that one-half of this was made necessary by the Troubles. Thus, we get a total cost of £8.4 billion (28 times £300 million).

The total economic cost of the Troubles is therefore about £12 billion. Several objections might be lodged against such a figure. In the first place, it might be argued that the calculations are rather crude. Yes, they are, but to some degree the limited availability of data makes this inevitable. In any case, one could be confident that a much more detailed approach to the above components would almost certainly find a total of at least £10 billion and perhaps even one greater than £12 billion.

So far we have not attempted to make any allowance for the most obvious loss created by the Troubles in Northern Ireland namely, the 2,700 residents of the Province killed since 1969. (This does not include the 451 members of the Regular Army who have been killed whilst on duty in the

Province during 1969-February 1997.) For illustrative purposes, one could use the value of a human life estimated at £700,000[2] and employed by the UK Department of Transport in 1993 in its cost-benefit procedures. This would then imply an equivalent monetary value of £1.9 billion (2,700 times £700,000).

It is important to stress that all of these estimates apply to Northern Ireland by itself. The equivalent economic cost of violence in Great Britain, the Republic of Ireland and the rest of the world would almost certainly add several pounds billion more to the total. This may explain why our own estimate of 'the total cost of the Troubles' at £14 billion falls somewhat short of that of the estimate of £23.5 billion in Tomlinson (1995). Tomlinson's estimate seems to be on a UK-wide basis and includes an element for the additional costs of maintaining the Regular Army in Northern Ireland plus enlarged military intelligence.

Northern Ireland Economic Growth 1997 Onwards, How Big a 'Peace Dividend'?

If it proves a difficult exercise to estimate the scale of impact of political instability and violence during the past then it is doubly hazardous to try to quantify the possible economic upturn which might be occasioned by a return to peace. Since the work of Keynes (1936), and perhaps for longer, economists have regarded uncertainty as a major deterrent to investment. To the extent that political instability has increased the uncertainty faced by indigenous firms in Northern Ireland then the achievement of peace might be regarded as likely to lead to an increase in investment in that sector (e.g. locally owned manufacturers, firms and service companies). However, and notwithstanding some of the estimations shown in the previous section, it is not clear that the scale of the material damage done by violence in terms of bombed factories and offices and burnt lorries and equipment etc. was ever sufficiently large to have induced a substantial decline in investment levels in indigenously owned firms (investment rates in manufacturing exceeded those in Great Britain during much of the 1970s and 1980s (Hitchens, Wagner and Birnie, 1990; Hitchens and Birnie, 1994) though some of this could be attributed to externally controlled firms and the impact of the generous system of capital grants).

Table 8.3 Possible scale of employment effects of peace

	Employment effects (p.a.) over a 5-10 year period
Higher investment in indigenous firms	positive and small
Higher investment by external firms	no more than +1,000 p.a.
Increased tourism	+1,000 - 2,000 p.a. over ten years
Increased North-South trade	+700 p.a. over five years
EU and USA monies	+500 - 1,000 p.a. over five years
Decreased government spending (law and order)	-10,000 to 15,000 total decline

Source: Various sources drawing, for example, on the suggestions of such studies as Bradley (1996), Gudgin (1997) and Bew, Patterson and Teague (1997).

It seems much more likely that some jobs would be created once Northern Ireland's negative image problem has a reduced impact on flows of inward investment. However, even if Northern Ireland could double the in-flow of projects relative to the average in the first half of the 1990s the impact would still be quite small (Table 8.3). Tourism represents what would probably be the main source of gains to employment. In the mid-1990s it was projected that total employment might be doubled or more relative to a baseline of about 10,000 employed. This is critically dependent on there being an adequate expansion of physical capacity, e.g. hotel beds, and it also has to be assumed that the number and quality of visitor attractions in the region would be commensurate with this higher level of activity and also that any negative feedback occasioned through any environmental deterioration caused by increased tourist numbers could be contained (Chapter 3).

The estimate of the impact of increased North-South trade is based on the study of Scott and O'Reilly (1992) (see also Chapter 7) and is contingent on a doubling of cross-border sales in manufacturing. A number of additional transfer payments to Northern Ireland, from the EU and USA, were agreed in 1994 and these are likely to have small and positive employment effects in each year up to the end of the decade.

The main 'negative' employment effect of peace could be a run-down in the levels of employment in law and order and security. Various estimates of this impact have been made. The usual procedure has been to estimate Northern Ireland's normal or peace time law and order employment on the basis of either the number of police in 1969 or the size of the police force in some part of England of roughly similar population and extent of urbanistion (Bew, Patterson and Teague, 1997). Such estimations suggest that two-thirds to three-quarters of mid-1990s policing strength might be excess to peace time requirements. Once allowance is made for local employment within the Army and prison services, and also for any multiplier effects, then a reduction in employment of between 10,000 and 15,000 might take place as government spending on law and order was adjusted.

Perhaps the most important conclusion to be drawn from this exercise is that there is a positive or net gain but that this would be even after 10 years *not* very large (perhaps no greater than 10,000 additional jobs). The situation would be more favourable if it could be assumed that any public monies saved on spending on law and order were retained within some other section of the total Northern Ireland budget (e.g. to spend more on hospitals, schools or transport links). However, it does look unlikely that the Treasury in London would be prepared to allow the Northern Ireland spending block to enjoy any such peace dividend for more than two or three years.

Some Issues Which Remain Unresolved

Is peace a 'necessary' and/or 'sufficient' condition for economic progress? Perhaps the soundest conclusion is that peace is not sufficient by itself to generate any economc miracle. In Chapters 2 and 3 we traced the extent, nature and explanations of Northern Ireland's competitiveness problem at the sector level. One important implication of such analysis is that it demonstrates that many of Northern Ireland's economic problems in the late 1990s were very deep rooted. Some of them were present as early as the inter-war period and so it would be naive to expect that peace by itself would resolve some of these difficulties. At the same time, the record of the regional economy during the 1970s and 1980s and particularly since 1990 suggests that peace is not a necessary condition for a rate of progress which is moderate and sustained. However, in absence of permanent peace trend GDP growth is not likely to go much above 3 per cent annually and so the best that would be on offer would be slow convergence on UK or EU average.

Peace would improve things to the extent that more inward investment arrived and to the extent that this was of a higher quality (i.e. involving R&D spending and relatively high productivity). In the long run peace would also help to upgrade human capital. There would probably be less out-migration of highly qualified persons and conversely there would be more in-migration of those who have had wider experience.

Since the mid-1970s there has been much debate amongst economists as to whether the traditional view of economic growth, the so-called neoclassical growth theory (which stresses the simple accumulation of inputs of capital stock and labour) or the more recent endogenous growth theory (which claims that there can be increasing returns to the application of technology and human capital) better explains the post-1945 data on the growth of nations (Mankiw, Romer and Weil, 1992; Barro and Sala-i-Martin, 1995; Landes, 1998). A crude summary of the state of the debate so far might be to say that economists have discovered that good and efficient government, stable institutions and peace are likely to promote economic growth. Perhaps one should say these results have been rediscovered by economists because they would hardly have surprised Adam Smith 220 years ago.[3] The application to Northern Ireland is obvious.

Would a return to a regional administration improve policy making? There is at least a fair probability that the medium term future in Northern Ireland will be considerably more peaceful than the 1969-95 period, there is also now (May 1998) the possibility that substantial policy making powers are going to be given to a regional administration. To have as many decisions as possible taken by locally elected representatives might be considered as desirable in its own right but what would be the impact on the local economy?

Under the devolved Stormont Parliament (1921-72) Northern Ireland did have some powers to exercise in terms of industrial policy. There were the New Industries (Development) Acts of 1932 and 1937 though these industrial development efforts were not any greater than in the Special Development Areas of Great Britain. Apart from the establishment of Short Brothers in the Belfast Harbour area after 1936, which might have happened anyway given that site's very strong locational attractions to the aircraft company (the availability of skilled labour, cheap land and an airport runway), only 279 jobs were created through financial inducements

(Johnson, 1985). One independent Unionist MP in the Stormont Parliament of the 1930s enquired whether, 'If the Government set up a few new chip shops they would not give more jobs' (Buckland, 1979). Nesbitt (1995) argued that Northern Ireland suffered during 1921-72 because it was being excluded from the main councils of decision making in the London Government and civil service. What was certainly true was that the devolved Stormont Parliament was always handicapped by its lack of fiscal resources (Wilson, 1955).

A consideration of the previous experience of devolved economic policy making need not indicate what the future will be like under any new Assembly. In the short to medium term it does not seem likely that the Assembly will have much power to vary the total amount of spending and taxation in Northern Ireland relative to the base line previously established by the UK Exchequer (a contrast can be drawn with the Scottish Parliament). Some commentators (Gibson, 1996) have seen this a major limitation on the likely efficiency of the delivery of public services in Northern Ireland. However, the Assembly will start off with a much bigger block of total spending than was available to the old Stormont Parliament and will presumably be able to quite quickly begin to make distributional adjustments between Departments. It remains to be seen how well the local political parties would exercise their stewardship over such resources. Over the last 25 years they have had little experience of administering anything above the local government level. We can only guess at what, say, an Ulster Unionist Economy Minister might do, or an SDLP Health Minister or, even, a Sinn Fein Education Minister (for different views on the relationship between economic ideology and unionism and nationalism see Birnie (1998) and Michie and Sheehan (1998)).

In principle the Assembly, along with the Executive of Ministers, could lead to quicker and more flexible decision making (this advantage has also been claimed for the prospective devolved Scottish Parliament, Ashcroft (1998)). In practice this will depend on how often its complex system of checks and balances is called into play, the arithmetic of party representation, and whether there is now some sort of practical consensus between the Ulster Unionist Party and SDLP on getting on with the job of running Northern Ireland. If, and it is a big if, the arrangements did work then there could be indirect and positive impacts on the economy. A generalised sense of goodwill probably would have some, albeit unquantifiable, impact on investment. Emigration of the highly skilled might be decreased (particularly of those 18-21 years old, usually from a Protestant and unionist background, who are currently leaving in large numbers to study at universities in England and Scotland and most of whom do not return).

The 10 April 1998 Agreement, which was endorsed by the 22 May 1998 Referendum, tied the success or otherwise of the internal Assembly to the so-called 'Strand Two' or North-South relationships. The economic impact of the latter are unclear. As Chapter 7 outlined, much of the mutually beneficial economic, social and cultural co-operation is probably already occurring in any case. The proposed North-South Ministerial Council formalises this situation and the examples quoted in the Agreement as areas for possible further joint action, such as animal health, suggest the extent and impact of any development in the medium term could be quite limited. Once again, the main economic impacts may be subtle, indirect and unquantifiable. If the extent of cross-border links envisaged in the document does prove sufficient to cause a significant proportion of the nationalist population to feel at ease with a Northern Ireland within the UK, and if peace and stability are attained, then there may be the beginnings of that degree of community trust, or a civic society, which some commentators have seen as foundational to economically successful regions elsewhere in Europe (Fukuyama, 1995; Dunford and Hudson, 1996).

Both now and forever a green and pleasant region? The UK Government, like its counterparts around the world, now declares that economic growth has to be sustainable That is, GDP increase should not be bought at the price of degradation of environmental assets which may be very valuable or indeed priceless in a social sense and yet often do not have any market price attached to their use. It has even been claimed that 'green' virtue brings its own reward in that companies which pay attention to environmental issues are likely to boost profits through better management of resources as well as the spur given to innovation (Porter, 1990; Palmer, Oates and Portney, 1995; Porter and Linde, 1995). This approach to policy making also appears to have strongly influenced Northern Ireland (DED, 1993).

In fact, it is often claimed that the quality of the environment has been and is likely to remain one of Northern Ireland's principal competitive advantages (Department of the Environment, 1998). It is possible to see how this perception has been created. Northern Ireland has a relatively low density of population. There are few extractive or heavy industries. The main types of farming, dairying and beef, have left much of the countryside looking attractive (for example, small fields with hedge rows). Outside of Belfast and Londonderry the urban centres are mostly small and have usually maintained their character. In reality, however, the quality of the physical environment is much more mixed.

Unlike the rest of the UK or, indeed, the Republic of Ireland, there are as of yet no plans for an independent Environmental Protection Agency in Northern Ireland. This implies a bizarre situation where the poacher and gamekeeper potentially may be the same. The Department of Environment has responsibility for prosecuting any private sector organisation which pollutes rivers and produces large scale fish kills. Its own water and sewerage agency sometimes causes such pollution. The application of polluter pays principles in terms of charging firms for water use and cleansing has in fact lagged Great Britain (Hitchens, Birnie, McGowan, Triebswetter and Cottica, 1998). Similarly, the application of legislation to meet EU Directives on recycling packaging waste has lagged behind the rest of the UK (Hitchens, Birnie, Triebswetter and Bertossi, 1998). Water quality and recycling standards may be somewhat above those currently in place in the Republic of Ireland but both Irish economies are still behind EU best practice. During the 1970s and 1980s a very relaxed view appears to have been taken with respect to allowing planning permission for the building of dwellings in the countryside. One result may have been a possibly unsightly sprawl of 'Spanish villas' on most of the vistas off the main roads across the Province.

There is a very strong suspicion that the Republic of Ireland at one stage engaged in a toxic trade off whereby environmental degradation was accepted as part of the cost of reliance on inward investment by 'dirty' chemical firms (Keohane, 1989; Jacobson and Andreosso, 1990). Similarly Northern Ireland has at least the possibility to use a relatively lax environmental policy to be a sort of industrial development policy in disguise. (This potential is partly the product of the fact that under the Direct Rule system of government legislation for Northern Ireland tends to lag behind that for the rest of the UK by at least a couple of years; it remains to be seen whether the introduction of the Northern Ireland Assembly will remove this gap.) If it has been the case that lower environmental standards have been accepted in Northern Ireland in the hope that this would maintain competitiveness, and further research is necessary to consider this point, then this might be one example of the myth of Northern Ireland exceptionalism. That is, because of the Troubles it was wrongly assumed that Northern Ireland would have to get by with something much less than UK or EU environmental standards.

There are at least three objections to this state of affairs. First, is it moral? Given that any such policy, if one has existed, has never been transparent we do not know if a majority of the public would consent to 'buy' GDP or employment gains at cost of environmental losses. Some of those loses could be very serious. Belfast is, for example, one of Europe's most polluted cities in terms of various air particles (Stanners and Bourdeau, 1995). There is growing evidence in Great Britain of the health impact of car exhaust emissions. As of yet, there has been no attempt to quantify the public health impact in the Greater Belfast area but it is likely to be considerable. (There are associated distributional aspects given that such environmental costs probably fall especially heavily on the poor.) Second, any such policy would be self-defeating in the medium to longer term. As recent official policy statements have often recognised, a heavily polluted Northern Ireland countryside is not likely, for example, to attract tourists and neither will it be able to produce the sorts of food products demanded by increasingly health and environmentally conscious consumers (Department of the Environment, 1998). Third, environmental regulations coming down from London or Brussels (Chapter 5) will increasingly constrain Northern Ireland to meet higher standards in any case.

It is undeniable that there are some trade-offs between industrial competitiveness and performance and environmental outcomes (Hitchens, 1998) but it is not clear that Northern Ireland has so far got the balance right. What is certain is that more research is need to generate the data necessary to conclude how far environmental standards lag behind best practice in the EU and what would be the likely impact on company competitiveness (and hence on output and jobs) of any attempt to raise those standards.

The last bastion of state planning? The Multi-Party Agreement of 10 April 1998 included the following declaration:

> Subject to the public consultation currently under way, the British Government will make rapid progress with:
> (i.) a new regional development strategy for Northern Ireland, for consideration in due course by the Assembly, tackling the problems of a divided society and social cohesion in urban, rural and border areas, protecting and enhancing the environment, producing a new approach to transport issues, strengthening the physical infrastructure of the region, developing the advantages and resources of rural areas and rejuvenating major urban centres;
> (ii.) a new economic development strategy for Northern Ireland, for consideration in due course by the Assembly which would provide for short and medium term economic planning linked as appropriate to the regional development strategy.. (p. 19).

Given the small size of the Northern Ireland economy (a total population smaller than that of some of the English conurbations and a total level of manufacturing employment smaller than the employment size of the big global corporations) it is perhaps not surprising that commentators often lapse into descriptions of Northern Ireland as one collective unit which can somehow be subject to a single forward plan. Sometimes this way of thought develops into one of thinking of a 'Northern Ireland PLC' which might do what Singapore or Japan has allegedly done with respect to picking winning sectors and so forth. Northern Ireland's Department of the Environment has been so bold as to propose a Regional Strategic Framework which includes a physical planning approach to the region predicated on assumptions as to GDP, employment growth and the development of housing and commuting patterns. Similarly, the Department of Economic Development is attempting to formulate a forward strategy which may emphasise particular sectors or even clusters of firms for selective policy assistance.

The sentiments contained within these planning approaches are admirable. Obviously both of these Northern Ireland Departments cannot avoid making certain assumptions about wider developments in the economy as they come to select policies for the future. One can also hope that the stewardship of Northern Ireland's physical environment over the next 25 years will represent clear progress relative to what was attained in the past. However, one is entitled to introduce some notes of caution regarding this upsurge in regional planning.

First, Northern Ireland has had many regional economic and physical development plans since the early 1960s. The extent of the positive impact on the economy of these plans remains unclear. An often centralised and non-accountable system of environmental planning has, for example, not always been accompanied by much by way of an improved environment (see the previous section). Second, there seems to be an emphasis on indicative planning in Northern Ireland which is now rarely observed elsewhere in the western economies. This begs a number of questions. Will planning work in Northern Ireland when it has been perceived to have failed elsewhere? If the planning has the apparently modest objective of removing obstacles to growth such as market failure, is there any evidence that the Northern Ireland authorities can successfully second guess the market? Third, past experience suggests that plans will often be knocked off course by unexpected events and so unrealistic plans impose serious economic costs. Consider, for example, the impact of the 1973 oil price rise on the 1960s man-made fibres inward investment policy, or how the start of the Troubles and the decline of Belfast City's population undermined the relevance of the Matthew's 'stop line' and the associated decentralisation of population to Craigavon and other centres, the shift of Northern Ireland's power stations to oil burning ahead of the 1970s oil shocks and the investment of Harland and Wolff into building a supertanker dry dock just before the collapse of the world oil market, and so on. (Admittedly, some of these examples of 'planning overtaken by events' relate as much to private sector as public sector decisions.)

We would recommend that the Northern Ireland Departments consider a range of possible scenarios and then produce summaries of possible policy responses to each of these scenarios. This procedure could then be opened up so as to ensure a more informed public and political debate as to what the most probable future is and how Northern Ireland can best adapt to external circumstances. Above all we would stress the maximum degree of flexibility should be built into policy making. That is, as far as is possible, policy makers should avoid producing sunk costs; that is, investments which are irreversible if they prove inappropriate. As one authority on the international history of comparative economic growth puts it, 'We must cultivate a sceptical faith, avoid dogma, listen and watch well, try to clarify ends, the better to choose means' (Landes, 1998).

Economics as it is often taught, even by these authors, perhaps over simplifies the behaviour of consumers and firms as the response to fixed and known technologies and preferences. In reality, technologies and preferences are in continual flux and are often unclear to economic agents.

The neo-Austrian perspective on economic activity as a discovery process (Kirzner, 1997) whereby new markets, processes and products are continually being uncovered by profit seeking entrepreneurs has some validity. How far government can produce flexibility and entrepreneurial behaviour remains unclear but it probably has some role as a facilitator (Porter, 1990).

None of this is deny the validity of *some* state planning within certain areas such as transport and the location of housing development where the externalities are substantial (according to one projection 200,000 houses will have to be built during the 1995-2020 period (Department of the Environment, 1998)). However, even in such cases the efficacy and cost effectiveness of such intervention could be improved by use of market instruments as opposed to more traditional controls. For example, congestion and use of cars in the Greater Belfast area could be discouraged by application of road price charging perhaps allied with a selective property development tax (perhaps set at a higher rate along the main southern commuter approaches to the City). Unfortunately, measures such as these would prove politically unpopular and there is a possibility that the new Northern Ireland Assembly would duck such options.

European and North-South developments Northern Ireland is a small regional economy within the EU. The development of the single market should have dynamic effects on growth (see Chapter 6). On the minus side some foreign direct investment may now be diverted to eastern Europe. From 1999 onwards Northern Ireland will probably lose its Objective One status with respect to assistance and there would be a corresponding reduction in monies received from the Structural and other EU funds.

In a static sense the gain from net EU receipts was equivalent to about 2-4 per cent of Northern Ireland's GDP in the mid-1990s (see Chapter 5) compared to a net gain to the Republic of Ireland at that time of 6-8 per cent.

EMU, if and when the UK participates, should reduce transaction costs. Moreover, exchange rate risk would be reduced with respect to trading and investment flow within the 'Euro-land' area. To the extent there is an improvement in general European macroeconomic conditions, then Northern Ireland could be pulled upwards by trade effects. One estimate has been that UK membership of EMU could boost Northern Ireland's GDP by 1 per cent and employment by 8,000 (NIEC, 1998c) (these impacts being of a similar proportional order of magnitude to those forecast for the Republic of Ireland economy if the UK were to join relative to the now much more likely scenario of, 'Republic of Ireland in, and UK out', by the Economic and Social Research Institute's model of the Republic of Ireland economy) .

On the other hand, many macroeconomists reckon that the adjustment process to meet the Maastricht criteria for EMU has already had a deflationary impact throughout the EU. In the longer term, EMU would entail a loss of control over monetary and fiscal policy and hence the ability to fix instruments such as interest rates, public deficits and exchange rates appropriate to national/regional conditions.

Northern Ireland is the only UK region with a land frontier and its immediate neighbour is likely to join the first stage of EMU. There will therefore be the potential for disruption to cross-border trade and EU agricultural price support policies as Northern Ireland stays 'out' but the Republic of Ireland goes 'in' during the 1999-2002 period. However, these costs of opting out may still be outweighed by the 'option value' of waiting to see how well the Euro works in the first couple years after January 1999. We have argued in any case (see Chapter 7) that the conceivable economic gains from greater economic integration of the two Irish economies are likely to be relatively modest. Michie and Sheehan (1998) place more stress on what might be gained through closer harmonisation of the two economies though they seem to imply that this would require extensive adjustment of Northern Ireland's constitutional relationship with both the rest of the UK and with the Republic of Ireland (probably a much greater move towards all-Ireland forms of government and administration than that which is likely to follow from the 10 April 1998 Agreement).

In Chapter 2 we considered the possibility that some of the greatest gains to North-South co-operation might be realised at the level of the firm. Notably by Northern Ireland companies (usually very small by European standards) merging with or forming other links with Republic of Ireland counterparts (sometimes much larger) (Bradley, 1996). Certainly, there is room for much more research on the nature and extent of inter-firm linkages across the island (and the extent to which the border constitutes a friction to these). Such links do not necessarily require all-Ireland political or administrative structures though they are unlikely to assisted by the separate development of the two currency areas. It is also worth repeating a note of caution we sounded on an earlier occasion. Indigenously owned firms on both sides of the Irish border often have relatively low productivity levels (Hitchens and Birnie, 1997). Alliances between Northern Ireland and Republic of Ireland companies might therefore be a case of the blind leading the blind.

Educational issues To an even greater extent than the rest of the UK, Northern Ireland now has mass higher education (more than one-third of those aged 18-21 years go to university). Some might question whether this is in principle a wholly good thing. However, that question may be beside the point in that this is the situation we are already in and there is unlikely to be a change back to the previous elite view of higher education. A more immediately relevant question for policy makers is how spending on, and provision of, third level education could be adjusted to maximise economic benefits. Should, for example, more university places be provided within the region to try to stem the outmigration of 18 year old students? The answer might appear to be yes in order to reduce what has been seen as an erosion of Northern Ireland's potential level of human capital in the future. On the other hand, expansion of graduate numbers would not necessarily or immediately be translated into greater use of graduates within the employed labour force. According to some informed sources the unemployment rate for Northern Ireland graduates in late 1997-early 1998 was already relatively high.

There continue to be difficulties with respect to technical and vocational education. It is reckoned that that the extent of inequality in the distribution of income and wealth in Northern Ireland exceeds that of Great Britain (Harris, 1990). Some commentators have argued that there is scope to use public spending on schooling at the primary and secondary levels to increase equality of opportunity. It has also been argued that there would be extensive private and social benefits from the increased provision of nursery education (Moser, 1997).

What is the relationship between growth and equity? Should issues of poverty and distribution be held back until after higher growth had already been achieved or are the social conditions best seen as a precondition for growth? This is a pressing question since, at the time of writing, the government has declared its intention to place 'equality' and 'Targeting Social Need' considerations very high within its policy priorities.

Similarly, the multi-Party Agreement concluded on 10 April 1998 placed great stress on so-called social inclusion.

A number of recent commentators have argued that the Northern Ireland economy would perform much better if there was much wider social trust and cohesion (Dunford and Hudson, 1996). This is undoubtedly true but begs the question how far any perceived lack of legitimacy of the status quo derives from political/constitutional as opposed to social/economic factors. That is, could any such alienation be remedied by economic changes in any case. Although in the long run equity and growth can conceivably go together, in the short run there may be trade-offs. For example, the requirement to meet social needs criteria in the distribution of public spending could conceivably reduce the efficiency of the delivery of such spending. Similarly, as was noted in Chapter 2, the stringent Fair Employment legislation undoubtedly poses some costs on Northern Ireland employers in terms of reduced ease and flexibility of recruitment procedures. It is also possible that frictional unemployment is increased to the extent that the unemployed in Northern Ireland, unlike their counterparts elsewhere cannot use the normal, often informal methods of job search and application for vacancies (Borooah and Forsythe, 1997).

Another equity-efficiency trade-off might be created by the introduction of the national minimum wage from 1999 onwards. The Low Pay Commission has set its face against any regional variation in the statutory minimum. According to a range of measures the incidence of 'low pay' in Northern Ireland is substantially greater than in Great Britain (NIEC, 1998a). To the extent that many sectors in Northern Ireland have comparatively low productivity, are labour intensive and produce products or services which are unsophisticated and compete primarily on cost, then in the short run at least the minimum wage will be a negative shock to competitiveness. The Northern Ireland Assembly could not exercise a regional opt-out from the minimum wage and it is unlikely it would want to. The optimists may claim that the long run effect will be beneficial in the sense that Northern Ireland companies will be forced to upgrade to higher quality products. This may be too sanguine a view but at least is emphasises the need for policy makers to focus on measures which could help to promote this outcome.

High public spending: Blessing or a bane? Public spending does boost aggregate demand and hence maintains employment. It helps to uphold the parity principle with respect to levels of health and social welfare spending in Northern Ireland relative to Great Britain. It has been argued that the sudden removal of some of this funding would be a large and potentially catastrophic shock to the economy (Bew, Patterson and Teague, 1997). On the other hand, and especially if a long-term consideration is taken, a large public sector does have a cost in terms of the encouragement given to attitudes of dependency hence reducing enterprise (see Chapters 2 and 4). In the mid-1990s one unintended side effect of general UK fiscal stringency was that for the first time since the 1970s there was a substantial slow down in Northern Ireland public spending (indeed, by 1997/98 spending was forecast to fall in real term). This also implied a reduction in the state spending/GDP ratio, albeit that ratio would have to fall a very far way before Northern Ireland moved into line with the UK average. This slow reduction in the extent of dependence on the public sector was very much in line with the spirit of the competitiveness approach to regional economic development which was adopted during the 1990s (see below).

At the same time, the fiscal impact of the first year of the 1997 Labour Government has been to increase slightly public spending in real terms (by up to 2 per cent per annum) compared to the original base line projections. On 12 May 1998 the Chancellor of the Exchequer, Gordon Brown, announced a package of, '£315 million investment in the renewal and modernisation of Northern Ireland'. It was striking, though hardly surprising given the general 'New Labour' emphasis on encouraging so-called 'endogenous economic growth' through strengthening the supply side, how much of this extra spending fell under the types of headings identified in the various studies of the explanations of growth (Barro and Sala-i-Martin, 1995). For example, £65 million on upgrading skills and labour market flexibility (e.g. amongst the long term unemployed aged over 25) and £87 million on improving key road routes.[4] A further £21 million was devoted to the Innovation and Tourism Fund (this was to include part of the set-up cost of a new Science Park). More questionable given the previous experience of regional policy (see earlier in this Chapter) and, indeed, the priorities of the 1990s competitiveness strategy was the decision to give what will in effect be a large degree of capital subsidisation to Northern Ireland's small and medium sized enterprises (probably to be defined as any locally owned firm or substantially autonomous unit employing less than 250 persons in any sector) in the form of 100 per cent first year capital allowances (worth £100 million).

Changes in industrial/economic policy relating to the goal of competitiveness There may be two key questions in this regard. First of all, after the very mixed record during the 1950s-98 period how likely is it that the authorities in Northern Ireland will be able to devise a system of industrial policy which allow effective intervention without significant costs in terms of economic efficiency? Second, is the comparatively recent emphasis on clustering at all viable in practice?

The answer to the first question is still unclear. A previous book by the authors (Hitchens, Wagner and Birnie, 1990) indicated that Northern Ireland's competitiveness performance was relatively weak compared to both the UK average and international benchmarks, especially West Germany, at the end of the 1980s. It is significant that this current book indicates that the improvements in competitiveness performance in manufacturing, farming, producer services and tourism since 1990 have been small.

As to the second question, there may have been insufficient realisation amongst policy makers that successful clusters can only develop in certain socio-economic environments; for example, the high trust societies identified by Fukuyama (1995)). Northern Ireland may not yet have one of those environments.

Conclusion Our summary of the economic policy agenda for the Assembly has inevitably been selective and yet we could argue the items listed are likely to be the main ones needing attention. Of course, the main focus of interest will be how far the Assembly can resolve the disagreement between the Northern Ireland Parties on constitutional issues. However, if the Assembly does begin to successfully deal with the broader government of Northern Ireland then the agenda presented in this Chapter will be highly relevant.

Notes

1. **Table 8.4 Deaths and injuries in Northern Ireland attributed to the Troubles, 1969 to 1995**

	Deaths	Injuries
1969	14	765
1970	25	811
1971	174	2,592
1972	470	4,876
1973	252	2,651
1974	250	2,398
1975	247	2,474
1976	297	2,729
1977	112	1,387
1978	81	985
1979	113	875
1980	76	801
1981	101	1,350
1982	97	525
1983	77	510
1984	64	866
1985	55	916
1986	61	1,450
1987	95	1,130
1988	94	1,047
1989	62	959
1990	76	906
1991	94	962
1992	85	1,066
1993	84	824
1994	61	825
1995	9	937
1969-95	3,196	37,617

Source: Northern Ireland Statistics and Research Agency (1997).

Table 8.4 records the number of deaths and injuries attributed to 'political violence' during 1969-95 (that is, from the start of the current 'Troubles' through to the first of the mid-1990s ceasefires). An alternative data source,

The Cost of the Troubles Study, at INCORE, University of Ulster, suggests a higher total death toll in Northern Ireland; 3,600 between 1969 and mid-1998 (The Times, 1998, May 14). Ninety-one per cent of these being men and 74 per cent under 40. Of those killed, 53 per cent were civilians with no connection to the security forces of paramilitary organisations. Nearly 29 per cent were serving members of the security forces, half from outside Northern Ireland, 12.5 per cent were republican paramilitaries and 3 per cent loyalist paramilitaries. Some 87 per cent of the dead were killed by paramilitaries (59 per cent by republicans, 28 per cent by loyalists) and 11 per cent by the security forces. Between 40,000 and 50,000 people were injured according to the INCORE estimates.

2. For an international comparison of the 'value of a human life' and a description of the Department of Transport method see Maunder, Myers, Walls and Le Roy, 1995, p. 184. For an alternative and lower valuation placed on life see Sloman ,1995, p. 439.
3. 'Commerce and manufactures can seldom flourish long in any state which does not enjoy a regular administration of justice; in which the people do not feel themselves secure in the possession of their property...' Adam Smith, *The Wealth of Nations*, Book V, Chapter 3.
4. The particular road improvements were to be: West link and motorway bridges, £35 million; Belfast-Larne, £10 million; Loughbrickland-Newry, £15 million; Antrim-Ballymena, £7 million; Londonderry-Ballygawley, £12 million and the Toome bypass, £8 million.

Bibliography

van Ark, B. (1992), 'Comparative Productivity in British and American Manufacturing', *National Institute Economic Review*, no. 142, pp. 63-73.

van Ark, B. (1993), *International Comparisons of Output and Productivity: Manufacturing Productivity Performance of Ten Countries from 1950 to 1990*, Monograph Series, no. 1, Growth and Development Centre, Groningen.

van Ark, B. (1994a), *Comparative Output and Productivity in Spanish Manufacturing 1950-1989*, mimeo, Growth and Development Centre, Groningen.

van Ark, B. (1994b), *Reassessing Growth and Comparative Levels of Performance in Eastern Europe: The Experience of Manufacturing in Czechoslovakia and east Germany*, paper to Third EACES Conference, Budapest, 8-10 September.

Armstrong, H. and Taylor, J. (1993), *Regional Economics and Policy*, Harvester Wheatsheaf, London, England.

Ashcroft, B. (1998), 'The Economic Possibilities for a Scottish Parliament', *Regional Studies*, vol. 32, no. 2, pp. 175-80.

Bailly, A. and Maillet, D. (1988), *Le Secteur Tertiare en Question*, Economica, Paris.

Banking Ireland (1992), 'Belfast-Dublin New Economic Axis', 23 September, Dublin.

Barnett, C. (1986), *The Audit of War: The Illusion and Reality of Britain as a Great Power*, Macmillan, London.

Barrett, S. (1995), 'The Culliton Report - Three Years On', *Irish Banking Review*, Spring, pp. 43-51.

Barro, R. and Sala-i-Martin, X. (1991), 'Convergence Across States and Regions', *Brookings Papers on Economic Activity*, no. 1, pp. 107-58.

Barro, R. and Sala-i-Martin, X. (1995), *Economic Growth,* McGraw-Hill, New York.

Barton, B. (1995), *Northern Ireland in the Second World War,* Northern Ireland Historical Society, Belfast.

Baumol, W.J., Blackman, S.A.B. and Wolff, E.H. (1989), *Productivity and American Leadership*, MIT Press, Cambridge, MA.

BBC/RTE (1992), *Tourism*, Programme in Route 92 Series, first shown on RTE1 6 May and BBC1 11 May, River Run Television, Dublin.

Belfast Telegraph (1998), *Northern Ireland's Top 500*, 18 February.

Bew, P., Patterson, H. and Teague, P. (1997), *Between War and Peace*, Lawrence and Wishart, London.

Birnie, J.E. (1994), *Irish and British Industrial Labour Productivity Levels*, Department of Economics Working Paper no. 47, Queen's University of Belfast.

Birnie, J.E. (1996), 'Comparative Productivity in Ireland: The Impact of Transfer Pricing and Foreign Ownership', in K. Wagner and B. van Ark (eds), *International Productivity Differences Measurement and Explanations*, Elsevier, Amsterdam, pp. 195-223.

Birnie, J.E. (1997), 'Irish Farming Labour Productivity: Comparisons with the UK, 1930s-1990', *Irish Economic and Social History*, XXIV, pp. 21-41.

Birnie, J.E. (1998), 'Orange, Green and in the Red: An Economic Audit of Unionism and Nationalism', in P.J. Roche and B. Barton. (eds), *Nationalism and Unionism in Ireland*, Ashgate, Aldershot (forthcoming).

Birnie, J.E. and Hitchens, D.M.W.N. (1996), *Northern Ireland Manufacturing Productivity Compared to Great Britain, 1980-92*, paper presented to ESRC Urban and Regional Studies Group Conference, Queen's University Belfast, 16 December.

Birnie, J.E. and Hitchens, D.M.W.N. (1998), 'Productivity and Income Per Capita Convergence in a Peripheral European country: The Irish Experience', *Regional Studies*, vol. 32, no. 3, pp. 223-34.

Black, J.B.H. (1987), 'Conciliation or Conflict', *Industrial Relations Journal*, vol. 18, no. 1, pp. 14-25.

Black, J.B.H. (1993), 'Industrial Relations Under Competition', *Review of Employment Topics*, vol. 1, no. 1, pp. 17-36.

Black, J.B.H. (1997), *Workers at War: Northern Ireland Industrial Relations in World War Two*, paper given to Queen's University Department of Economics and Northern Ireland Economic Research Centre Seminar Series, Queen's University Belfast, 14 November.

Borooah, V. and Forsythe, F.P. (1997), *Unemployment, Inactivity and Male Joblessness: The Northern Ireland, Labour Market in a Comparative Context*, paper presented to The Two Economies - North and South Conference, Stormont Hotel, Belfast, 28 February.

Borooah, V. and Lee, K. (1991), 'The Regional Dimension of Competitiveness in Manufacturing: Productivity, Employment and Wages in Northern Ireland and the UK', *Regional Studies*, vol. 25, no. 3, pp. 219-29.

Borooah, V., McKee, P., Heaton, N. and Collins, G. (1995), 'Catholic-Protestant Income Differences in Northern Ireland', *Review of Income and Wealth*, series 41, no. 1, pp. 41-56.

Boyle, G.E., Kearney, B., McCarthy, T. and Keane, M. (1991), *The Competitive Advantage of Irish Agriculture*, mimeo, Maynooth College, Kildare.

Bradley, J. (1996), 'Exploring Long-term Economic and Social Consequences of Peace and Reconciliation in the Island of Ireland', *Forum for Peace and Reconciliation Consultancy Studies*, no. 4, Stationery Office, Dublin.

Bradley, J. and McCartan, J. (1998), 'EMU and Northern Ireland Manufacturing', in NIEC, J. Bradley (ed.), *Regional Economic and Policy Impacts of EMU: The Case of Northern Ireland*, Research Monograph, no. 6, Northern Ireland Economic Council, Belfast, pp. 197-270.

Broadberry, S.N. (1994), 'Manufacturing and the Convergence Hypothesis: What the Long Run Data Show', *Journal of Economic History*, vol. 53, no. 4, pp. 772-95.

Buckland, P. (1979), *Factory of Grievances: Devolved Government in Northern Ireland 1921-39*, Gill and Macmillan, Dublin.

Cambridge Econometrics (1996), *Regional Economic Forecasts*, Cambridge Econometrics, Cambridge.

Cambridge Econometrics (1997), *Regional Economic Forecasts*, Cambridge Econometrics, Cambridge.

Canning, D., Moore, B. and Rhodes, J. (1987) , 'Economic Growth in Northern Ireland: Problems and Prospects', in P. Teague (ed.), *Beyond the Rhetoric*, Lawrence and Wishart, London, pp. 211-35.

Caskie, P., Davis, J. and Papadas, C. (1998), *The Impact of BSE on the Economy of Northern Ireland*, Centre for Rural Studies, Queen's University Belfast.

Cecchini, P. (1988), *The European Challenge 1992: The Benefits of a Single Market*, Wildwood House, Aldershot.

Clulow, R., and Teague, P. (1993), 'Governance structures and economic performance', in P. Teague (ed.), *The Economy of Northern Ireland*, Lawrence and Wishart, London, pp. 60-120.

CII (1990), *Newsletter*, May, Confederation of Irish Industry, Dublin.

Commission of the European Communities (1988), 'The Economics of 1992', *European Economy*, no. 35, Office for Official Publications of the European Communities, Luxembourg.

Commission of the European Communities (1992), *Panorama of EC Industry 1992-1993 Statistical Supplement*, Office for Official Publications of the European Communities, Luxembourg.

Commission of the European Communities (1993), *Panorama of EC Industry 1993*, Office for Official Publications of the European Communities, Luxembourg.

Commission of the European Communities (1994), *Panorama of EC Industry 1994*, Office for Official Publications of the European Communities, Luxembourg.

Commission of the European Communities (1996), *The Agricultural Situation in the European Union, 1995 Report*, Office for Official Publications of the European Communities, Luxembourg.

Compton, P. (1995), *Demographic Review Northern Ireland 1995*, Research Monograph no. 1, Northern Ireland Economic Council, Belfast.

Convery, F. (1992), 'Environment and Energy', in Government of Ireland, *Ireland in Europe A Shared Challenge*, Stationery Office, Dublin, pp. 175-97.

Crafts, N.F.R. (1984), 'Nineteenth Century Growth in Comparative Perspective', *Economic Perspectives,* vol. 36, p. 440.

Crafts, N.F.R. (1993), 'Can De-industrialisation Seriously Damage Your Wealth?', *Hobart Paper*, no. 120, Institute of Economic Affairs, London.

Crowley, J. (1992), 'Transport', in Government of Ireland, *Ireland in Europe A Shared Challenge*, Stationery Office, Dublin.

CSO (1987), *Annual Abstract of Statistics 1987*, Central Statistical Office, London.

CSO (1990), *Annual Abstract of Statistics 1990*, Central Statistical Office, London.

CSO (1995), *National Income and Expenditure 1995*, Government Publications, Dublin.

CSO (1996), *National Income and Expenditure 1996*, Government Publications, Dublin.

CSO and Irish Economic Association (1996), *Proceedings of Conference on Measuring Economic Growth*, CSO and IEA, Government Publications, Dublin.

Culliton (Report), (1992), otherwise known as the, *Report of the Industrial Policy Review Group*, Stationery Office, Dublin.

Daly, A., Hitchens, D.M.W.N and Wagner, K. (1985), 'Productivity, Machinery and Skills in a Sample of British and German Manufacturing Plants', *National Institute Economic Review*, no. 111, pp. 48-62.

Damesick, P.J. (1986), 'Service Industries, Employment and Regional Development in Britain: A Review of Recent Trends and Issues', *Trans. Inst. Br. Geogr.*, no. 11, pp. 212-26.

DANI (1997), *Statistical Review of Northern Ireland Agriculture 1996*, Economics and Statistics Division, Department of Agriculture Northern Ireland, Belfast.

D'Arcy, M. and Dickson, T. (1995), *Border Crossings Developing Ireland's Island Economy*, Gill and Macmillan, Dublin.

Davies, S.W. and Caves, R.E. (1987), *Britain's Productivity Gap*, Cambridge University Press, Cambridge.

Davis, J. (1991), *The Competitiveness of the Northern Ireland Dairy Sector*, Department of Agricultural and Food Economics, Queen's University Belfast.

Davis, J. (1998), *Agriculture and Rural Society in Northern Ireland: The Impact of EU Membership*, paper presented to Twenty-five Years On - The Impact of EU Membership on Northern Ireland Conference, Queen's University Belfast, 3 February.

DED (1987), *Pathfinder*, Department of Economic Development, Belfast.

DED (1990), *Northern Ireland Competing in the 1990s: The Key to Growth*, Department of Economic Development, Belfast.

DED (1995), *Growing Competitively a Review of Economic Development Policy in Northern Ireland*, Department of Economic Development, Belfast.

Denison, E.F. (1967), *Why Growth Rates Differ?*, Brookings Institute, Washington DC.

Department of Finance (1996), *Economic Review and Outlook*, Government Publications, Dublin.

Department of the Environment (1998), *Shaping our Future Towards a Strategy for the Development of the Region*, Department of the Environment for Northern Ireland, Belfast.

Department of Transport (1990), *Transport Statistics Great Britain 1979-1989*, Department of Transport, London.

Department of Transport (1991), *Transport Statistics Great Britain 1991*, Department of Transport, London.

Dertouzous, M.L., Lester, R.K. and Solow, R.M. (1989), *Made in America: Regaining the Productive Edge*, MIT Press, Cambridge MA.

DFP (1993), *Northern Ireland Structural Funds Plan 1994-1999*, Technical Supplement, Department of Finance and Personnel, Belfast.

Dignan, A. (1994), *Cost Competitiveness and Manufacturing Output Growth: The UK Regions in the 1980s*, paper presented to QUB Department of Economics/NIERC Joint Seminar Series, Belfast, 28 October.

DTI (1983), *Regional Industrial Development*, Cmnd 9111, HMSO, London.

DTI (1995), *Competitiveness: Forging Ahead*, Department of Trade and Industry, London.

DTI (1996), *Competitiveness: Creating the Enterprise Centre of Europe*, Department of Trade and Industry, London.

Dunford, M. and Hudson, R. (1996), *Successful European Regions: Northern Ireland Learning from Others*, Research Monograph no. 3, Northern Ireland Economic Council, Belfast.

Economist (1996), *Mad Cows and Englishmen*, 30 March.

Economist (1996), *Burnt by the Steak*, 6 April.

Economist (1996), *Inward Investment Bribing for Britain*, 8 June.

Economist (1996), *Wales Won*, 13 July.

Economist (1996), *Sliding Scales*, 2 November.

Economist (1997), *Uncommercial Travellers*, 1 February.

Economist (1997), *The Future of the State*, 20 September.

Economist (1998), *Spain and Portugal Ever Closer, Inside Europe's Union?*, 14 February.

Enright, M. (1994), *Regional Clusters and Economic Development: A Research Agenda*, Working Paper 94-074, Harvard Business School.

Financial Times (1993), *Bombed Out in Belfast*, 28 October.

Financial Times (1994), *Can Europe Compete? The Challenge*, 24 February.

Financial Times (1998), *FT 500 1998*, 22 January.

Financial Times (1998), *One Man's Meat Crisis May Prove Another Man's Gain*, 16 March.

FitzGerald, J. (1997), *ESRI's Medium Term Review- Evidence of Economic Progress*, paper presented to The Two Economies - North and South Conference, Stormont Hotel, Belfast, 28 February.

Fitzpatrick, J. and McEniff, J. (1992), 'Tourism', in Government of Ireland, *Ireland in Europe A Shared Challenge*, Stationery Office, Dublin, pp. 119-52.

Fothergill, S. and Guy, N. (1990), *The Closure of Branch Plants in Manufacturing During the 1980s*, Northern Ireland Economic Research Centre Report, Belfast.

Fukuyama, F. (1995), *Trust*, Hamish Hamilton, London.

Furness, G.W. and Stainer, T.F. (1981), 'Economic Performance in Agriculture in Northern Ireland and the Irish Republic', *Annual Report on Research and Technical Work*, Department of Agriculture Northern Ireland, Belfast.

Gibson, N. 'Northern Ireland and Westminister: Fiscal Decentralisation. A Public Economics Perspective', in NIEC (1996*), Decentralised Government and Economic Performance in Northern Ireland*, Occasional Paper no. 7, Northern Ireland Economic Council, Belfast, pp. 10-89.

Gorecki, P. (1997), *Industrial Policy in Northern Ireland: The Case for Radical Reform*, paper presented to the Manchester Statistical Society, CIS Building, Manchester, 21 October.

Government of Ireland (1993), *Ireland National Development Plan 1994-1999*, Stationery Office, Dublin.

Gray, A.W. (1992), 'Industry and Trade', in Government of Ireland, *Ireland in Europe A Shared Challenge*, Stationery Office, Dublin, pp. 35-63.

Gripaios, P.A. and Gripaios, R.J. (1992), 'The UK and the European Super Regions: The Case of the Atlantic Arc', *European Research*, vol. 3, no. 3, pp. 12-15.

Gudgin, G. (1996), *The Macroeconomic Impact of European Community Structural Funds on Northern Ireland 1989-93*, NIERC Report, Northern Ireland Economic Research Centre, Belfast.

Gudgin, G. (1997), *The Northern Ireland Economy in the Year 2000*, paper presented to The Two Economies - North and South Conference, Stormont Hotel, Belfast, 28 February.

Gudgin, G. (1998), *Twenty-five years A'growing: The Impact of EC Membership on the Northern Ireland Economy 1973-97*, paper presented to Twenty-five Years On - The Impact of EU Membership on Northern Ireland Conference, Queen's University Belfast, 3 February.

Gudgin, G., Hart, M., Fagg, J., Keegan, R., and D'Arcy E. (1989), *Job Generation in Manufacturing Industry 1973-1986: A Comparison of Northern Ireland with the Republic of Ireland and the English Midlands*, NIERC Report, Northern Ireland Economic Research Centre, Belfast.

Hamilton, D. (1996), *Industrial Policy in Northern Ireland- Levels of Financial Assistance and the Selectivity of the IDB*, paper presented to ESRC Urban and Regional Studies Group Conference, Queen's University Belfast, 16 December.

Hansen, N. (1990), 'Do Producer Services Induce Regional Economic Development?', *Journal of Regional Science*, vol. 30, no. 4, pp. 465-76.

Harris, R.I.D. (1983), 'The Measurement of Capital Services in Production for the UK Regions 1968-78', *Regional Studies*, vol. 17, no. 3, pp. 169-80.

Harris, R.I.D. (1991), *Regional Economic Development Policy in Northern Ireland 1945-88*, Avebury, Aldershot.

Hayami, Y., Miller, B., Wade, W. and Yamashita, S. (1971), *An International Comparison of Production and Productivities*, Technical Bulletin, no. 27, University of Minnesota.

Henry, E.W. (1989), *The Capital Stock of Ireland*, General Research Series Paper, no. 145, Economic and Social Research Institute, Dublin.

Hindley, B. and Howe, M. (1996), *Better Off Out? The Benefits and Costs of EU Membership*, Institute of Economic Affairs, Paper no. 99, London.

Hitchens, D.M.W.N. (1998), 'Environmental Policy and the Implications for Competitiveness in the Regions of the EU', *Regional Studies*, vol. 31, no. 8, pp. 813-19.

Hitchens, D.M.W.N. and Birnie, J.E. (1993), 'Productivity and Economic Performance', in NESC, *Education and Training and Policies for Economic and Social Development*, Report no. 95, National Economic and Social Council, Dublin, pp. 36-95.

Hitchens, D.M.W.N. and Birnie, J.E. (1994), *The Competitiveness of Industry in Ireland*, Avebury, Aldershot.

Hitchens, D.M.W.N. and Birnie, J.E. (1997), 'The Potential for a Belfast-Dublin Economic Corridor', *Australasian Journal of Regional Studies*, vol. 2, no. 2, pp. 167-87.

Hitchens, D.M.W.N., Birnie, J.E., Hamar, J., Wagner, K. and Zemplinerova, A. (1995), *The Competitiveness of Industry in the Czech Republic and Hungary*, Avebury, Aldershot.

Hitchens, D.M.W.N., Birnie, J.E., McGowan, A., Cottica, A. and Triebswetter, U. (1998), *The Firm, Regulation and Competitiveness*, Edward Elgar, Aldershot.

Hitchens, D.M.W.N., Birnie, J.E., Triebswetter, U. and Bertossi, P. (1998), *Measuring The Competitiveness Effects of Environmental Compliance: The Importance of Regulation and Market Pressures*, Report to the Commission of the European Communities, Department of Economics, Queen's University Belfast (forthcoming).

Hitchens, D.M.W.N. and O'Farrell, P.N. (1987), 'The Comparative Performance of Small Manufacturing Firms in Northern Ireland and South East England', *Regional Studies*, vol. 21, no. 6, pp. 543-54.

Hitchens, D.M.W.N. and O'Farrell, P.N. (1988a), 'The Comparative Performance of Small Manufacturing Firms Located in South Wales and Northern Ireland', *Omega*, vol. 16, no. 5, pp. 429-38.

Hitchens, D.M.W.N. and O'Farrell, P.N. (1988b), 'The Comparative Performance of Small Manufacturing Firms Located in the Mid-West of Ireland and Northern Ireland', *Economic and Social Review*, vol. 19, no. 3, pp. 177-98.

Hitchens, D.M.W.N., O'Farrell, P.N. and Conway, C. (1996a), 'The Competitiveness of Business Services in the Republic of Ireland, Northern Ireland, Wales and South East England', *Environment and Planning A*, vol. 28, pp. 1299-313.

Hitchens, D.M.W.N., O'Farrell, P.N. and Conway, C. (1996b), 'The Comparative Performance of Business Services in Northern Ireland and the Republic of Ireland', *Urban Studies*, vol. 33, no. 7, pp. 1093-110.

Hitchens, D.M.W.N., Wagner, K. and Birnie, J.E. (1990), *Closing the Productivity Gap: A Comparison of Northern Ireland, the Republic of Ireland, Britain and West Germany*, Gower-Avebury, Aldershot.

Hitchens, D.M.W.N., Wagner, K. and Birnie, J.E. (1991), 'Improving Productivity Through International Exchange Visits', *Omega*, vol. 19, no. 5, pp. 361-68.

Hitchens, D.M.W.N., Wagner, K. and Birnie, J.E. (1992), 'Measuring the Contribution of Product Quality to Competitiveness: A Note on Theory and Policy', *Economic and Social Review*, vol. 23, no. 4, pp. 455-63.

HMSO (1996), *NI Expenditure Plans and Priorities 1996/97 to 1998/99*, Her Majesty's Stationery Office, London.

HM Treasury (1989), 'Productivity in the 1980s', *Economic Progress Report*, no. 201, pp. 4-5.

Hood, N.S. and Young, S. (1983), *Multinational Investment Strategies in the British Isles*, HMSO, London.

IDB (1991), *Forward Strategy 1991-93*, Industrial Development Board, Belfast.

Irish News (1997), *A Single Island Economy*, 26 March.

Isles, K.S. and Cuthbert, N. (1957), *An Economic Survey of Northern Ireland*, HMSO, Belfast.

Jacobson, D. and Andresso, B. (1990), 'Multinational Investment', in A. Foley and B. Mulreany (eds), *The Single European Market and the Irish Economy*, Institute of Public Administration, Dublin, pp. 307-34.

Johnson, D. (1985), 'The Northern Ireland Economy, 1914-39', in L. Kennedy. and P. Ollerenshaw (eds), *An Economic History of Ulster 1820-1939*, Manchester University Press, Manchester, pp. 184-223.

Keenan, P. (1977), 'Technical Education for Farmers', in *Symposium on Technical Education for Agriculture*, Council for Education Awards, Dublin.

Kennedy, K.A. (1993), 'Long-term Trends in the Irish Economy', *Irish Banking Review, Summer*, pp. 16-25.

Kennedy, K.A., Giblin, T. and McHugh, D. (1988), *The Economic Development of Ireland in the Twentieth Century*, Croom Helm, London.

Kennedy, M. (1997), 'Towards Co-operation: Seán Lemass and North-South Economic Relations', *Irish Economic and Social History*, vol. XXIV, pp. 42-61.

Keohane, K. (1989), 'Toxic Trade-off: The Price Ireland Pays for Industrial Development', *The Ecologist*, vol. 19, no. 2, pp. 144-6.

Keynes, J.M. (1936), *The General Theory of Employment, Interest and Money*, Macmillan, London.

Kingon, S. (1998), 'Commercial and Industrial Review', *Belfast Telegraph*, 28 March.

Kinsella, R. (1992), 'Financial Services', in Government of Ireland, *Ireland in Europe A Shared Challenge*, Stationery Office, Dublin, pp. 95-118.

Kirzner, I. (1997), 'How Markets Work: Disequilibrium, Entrepreneurship and Discovery', *Hobart Paper*, no. 133, Institute of Economic Affairs, London.

Landes, D. (1998), *The Wealth and Poverty of Nations*, Little Brown,

LEDU (1991), *Forward Thinking: LEDU's Corporate Plan 1989-1994*, Local Enterprise Development Unit, Belfast.

Lucas, R.E. (1988), 'On the Mechanics of Economic Development', *Journal of Monetary Economics*, vol. 22, pp. 3-42.

MacEnroe, G. and Poole, W. (1995), 'Manufacturing: Two plus Two Makes More Than Four', in M. D'Arcy and T. Dickson (eds), *Border Crossings*, Gill and Macmillan, pp. 110-12.

Maddison, A. (1991), *Dynamic Forces in Capitalist Development*, Oxford University Press, Oxford.

Maguire, C. (1979), *Research and Development in Ireland*, National Board for Science and Technology, Dublin.

Mankiw, G. , Romer, D. and Weil, D. (1992), 'A Contribution to the Empirics of Economic Growth', *Quarterly Journal of Economics*, no. 107, pp. 407-38.

Marquand, J. (1983), 'The Changing Distribution of Service Employment', in J.B. Goddard and A.G. Champion (eds), *The Urban and Regional Transformation of Britain*, Methuen, London, pp. 99-134.

Marshall, J.N. (1982), 'Linkages Between Manufacturing Industry and Business Services', *Environment and Planning A*, vol. 14, no. 1, pp. 523-40.

Marshall, J.N. (1988), *Services and Uneven Development*, Oxford University Press, Oxford.

Martin, R. and Tyler, P. (1992), 'The Regional Legacy', in J. Michie (ed.), *The Economic Legacy 1979-1992*, Academic Press, London, pp. 140-67.

Matthews, R.C.O. (1988), 'Research on Productivity and the Productivity Gap', *National Institute Economic Review*, no. 124, pp. 66-71.

Matthews, A. (1992), 'Agriculture and Natural Resources', in Government of Ireland, *Ireland in Europe A Shared Challenge*, Stationery Office, Dublin, pp. 65-93.

Maunder, P., Myers, D., Walls, N. and Le Roy Miller, R. (1995), *Economics Explained*, Collins Educational, London.

McGregor, P., Swales, K. and Yin, Y.P. (1998), 'EMU: The UK Regional Context', in NIEC, J. Bradley (ed.), *Regional Economic and Policy Impacts of EMU: The Case of Northern Ireland*, Research Monograph no. 6, Northern Ireland Economic Council, Belfast, pp. 77-142.

McGurnaghan, M. and Scott, S. (1981), 'Trade and Co-operation in Electricity and Gas', *Understanding and Co-operation in Ireland*, Paper IV, Co-operation North, Belfast and Dublin.

McKinsey, (1993), *Manufacturing Productivity*, McKinsey Global Institute, Washington DC.

Michie, J. and Sheehan, M. (1998), 'The Political Economy of a Divided Ireland', *Cambridge Journal of Economics*, vol. 22, pp. 243-59.

Moriarty, (1993), 'Response of the Task Force to the Culliton Report/Employment through Enterprise' *Response of the Government to the Culliton Report*, Stationery Office, Dublin.

Moser, Sir Claus (1997), *Reforming Education in the United Kingdom: The Vital Priorities*, Report, no. 120, Northern Ireland Economic Council, Belfast.

Munck, R. (1993), *The Irish Economy*, Pluto Press, London.

Murphy, A. (1994), *The Irish Economy - Celtic Tiger or Tortoise?*, Money Markets International Report, MMI, Dublin.

Murphy, A. (1996), *The Two Faced Economy*, Proceedings of Conference on Measuring Economic Growth, Central Statistics Office (Ireland) and Irish Economic Association, Dublin, pp. 17-32.

Nesbitt, D. (1995), *Unionism Restated*, Ulster Unionist Information Office, Belfast.

NESC (1976), *A Comparative Study of Output, Value Added and Growth in Irish and Dutch Agriculture*, Report no. 24, National Economic and Social Council, Dublin.

NESC (1979), *Policies to Accelerate Agricultural Development*, Report no. 40, National Economic and Social Council, Dublin.

NESC (1989), *Ireland in the European Community: Performance, Prospects and Strategy*, Report no. 88, National Economic and Social Council, Dublin.

NESC (1992a), *The Irish Economy in a Comparative Institutional Perspective*, Report no. 93, National Economic and Social Council, Dublin.

NESC (1992b), *The Impact of Reform of the Common Agricultural Policy*, Report, no. 92, National Economic and Social Council, Dublin.

NESC (1993a), *The Association Between Economic Growth and Employment Growth in Ireland*, Report no. 94, National Economic and Social Council, Dublin.

NESC (1993b), *A Strategy for Competitiveness, Growth and Employment*, Report no. 96, National Economic and Social Council, Dublin.

New Ireland Forum (1984), *Comparative Description of the Economic Structure and Situation, North and South*, Stationery Office, Dublin.

NIEC (1993a), *R&D Activity in Northern Ireland*, Report no. 101, Northern Ireland Economic Council, Belfast.

NIEC (1993b), *Northern Ireland and the Recent Recession: Cyclical Strength or Structural Weakness?*, Report no. 104, Northern Ireland Economic Council, Belfast.

NIEC (1994), *The Implications of Peripherality for Northern Ireland*, Report no. 111, Northern Ireland Economic Council, Belfast.

NIEC (1995), *Reforming the Educational System in Northern Ireland*, Occasional Paper no. 1, Northern Ireland Economic Council, Belfast.

NIEC (1996), *Decentralised Government and Economic Performance in Northern Ireland*, Occasional Paper no. 7, Northern Ireland Economic Council, Belfast.

NIEC (1997a), *Rising to the Challenge: The Future of Tourism in Northern Ireland*, Report no. 121, Northern Ireland Economic Council, Belfast.

NIEC (1997b), *The 1996 Budget: Implications for Northern Ireland*, Report no. 122, Northern Ireland Economic Council, Belfast.

NIEC (1997c), *Towards Resolving Long-term Unemployment in Northern Ireland. A Response to the Long-term Unemployment Consultation Document*, Occasional Paper no. 8, Northern Ireland Economic Council, Belfast.

NIEC (1997d), *Educational Achievement in Northern Ireland: Patterns and Prospects*, Research Monograph no. 4, Northern Ireland Economic Council, Belfast.

NIEC (1998a), *The Impact of a National Minimum Wage on the Northern Ireland Economy. A Response to the Low Pay Commission*, Occasional Paper no. 9, Northern Ireland Economic Council, Belfast.

NIEC (1998b), *Competitiveness and Industrial Policy in Northern Ireland*, Research Monograph no. 5, Northern Ireland Economic Council, Belfast.

NIEC (1998c), *Regional Economic and Policy Impacts of EMU: The Case of Northern Ireland*, (J. Bradley (ed.)) Research Monograph no. 6, Northern Ireland Economic Council, Belfast.

NIERC (1992), *Northern Ireland Exports Survey*, Northern Ireland Economic Research Centre Report, NIERC, Belfast.

NIERC/DED/IDB (1997), *Made in Northern Ireland. Sold to the World. Northern Ireland Sales and Exports 1994/95-1995/96*, Northern Ireland Economic Research Centre/Department of Economic Development/Industrial Development Board, Belfast.

NIGC (1994), *Conceptual Framework for Steering Group*, Northern Ireland Growth Challenge, Belfast.

NITB (1996), *1995-1996 Annual Report. It's the People That Make It*, Northern Ireland Tourist Board, Belfast.

Northern Ireland Statistics and Research Agency (1997), *Northern Ireland Annual Abstract of Statistics 1997*, no. 15, Belfast.

O'Farrell, P.N. and Hitchens, D.M.W.N. (1989), *Small Firm Competitiveness and Performance*, Gill and Macmillan, Dublin.

Office for National Statistics (1996), *Regional Trends 1996*, ONS, London.

Office for National Statistics (1997a), *Regional Trends 1997*, ONS, London.

Office for National Statistics (1997b), *Annual Abstract of Statistics*, ONS, London.

Office for National Statistics (1997c), *Labour Market Trends*, November, vol. 105, no. 11, S24- S29.

Ó'Gráda, C. and O'Rourke, K. (1995), 'Economic Growth: Performance and Explanation', in J.W. O'Hagan (ed.), *The Economy of Ireland*, Macmillan, pp. 198-226.

Ó'Gráda, C. and O'Rourke, K. (1996), 'Irish economic growth, 1945-88', in N. Crafts and G. Toniolo (eds), *Economic Growth in Europe Since 1945*, Cambridge University Press and Centre for Economic Policy Research, Cambridge, pp. 388-426.

Ó'Gráda, C. (1994), *Ireland A New Economic History 1780-1939*, Oxford University Press, Oxford.

O'Leary, B., Lyne, T., Marshall, T. and Rowthorn, B. (1993), *Northern Ireland Shared Authority*, Institute for Public Policy Research, London.

O'Mahony, M. (1992), 'Productivity Levels in British and German Manufacturing Industry', *National Institute Economic Review*, no. 138, pp. 46-63.

O'Mahony, M. (1993), 'Capital Stocks and Productivity in Industrial Nations' *National Institute Economic Review*, no. 145, pp. 108-17.

O'Malley, E. (1985), 'Industrial Development in the North and South of Ireland: Prospects for an Integrated Approach', *Administration*, vol. 33, no. 1.

O'Malley, E. (1989), *Industry and Economic Development: The Challenge for the Latecomer,* Gill and Macmillan, Dublin.

O'Malley, E., Kennedy, K.A. and O'Donnell, R. (1992), *The Impact of the Industrial Development Agencies*, Report by the Economic and Social Research Institute to the Industrial Policy Review Group, Stationery Office, Dublin.

van Ooststroom, H. and Maddison, A. (1984), *An International Comparison of Levels of Real Output and Productivity in Agriculture in 1975*, Memo no. 162, Institute of Economic Research, University of Groningen.

van Ooststroom, H. and Maddison, A. (1993), *The International Comparison Of Value Added, Productivity and Purchasing Power Parities an Agriculture*, Memo 536GD-1, Groningen Growth and Development Centre.

Osborne, R.D. (1985), *Religion and Educational Qualifications in Northern Ireland*, Research Paper no. 8, Fair Employment Agency, Belfast.

Paige, D. and Bombach G. (1959), *A Comparison of National Output and Productivity in the United Kingdom and United States*, Organisation for European Economic Co-operation, Paris.

PEIDA (Consultants) (1984), *Transport Costs in Peripheral Regions*, Department of Economic Development and Scottish Office, Belfast and Edinburgh.

Pollitt, M. (1997), *The Restructuring and Privatisation of the Electricity Supply Industry in Northern Ireland - Will it Be Worth it?*, DAE Working Papers Amalgamated Series no. 9701 (revised), Cambridge.

Porter, M. (1990), *The Competitive Advantage of Nations*, The Free Press, New York.

PPRU (1986), *Northern Ireland Annual Abstract of Statistics 1985*, Policy Planning and Research Unit, Belfast.

PPRU (1987), *Transport Costs*, Discussion Paper, Policy Planning and Research Unit, Belfast.

PPRU (1992), *Northern Ireland Annual Abstract of Statistics 1991*, Policy Planning and Research Unit, Belfast.

PPRU (1996), *Northern Ireland Annual Abstract of Statistics 1995*, Policy Planning and Research Unit, Belfast.

Prais, S.J. (1981), *Productivity and Industrial Structure*, Cambridge University Press, Cambridge.

Pryke, F. (1993), *Endogenous Development in a Global Context: The Scope for Industrial Districts*, International Labour Office, Geneva.

Romer, P. (1986), 'Increasing Returns and Long Run Economic Growth', *Journal of Political Economy*, vol. 94, no. 5, pp. 1002-37.

Roper, S. (1993), *Manufacturing Profitability in Northern Ireland*, NIERC Report, Northern Ireland Economic Research Centre, Belfast.

Roper, S. (1997), *The Principles of the New Competition: An Empirical Assessment of Ireland's Position*, Working Paper no. 27, Northern Ireland Economic Research Centre, Belfast.

Roper, S. and Hoffman, H. (1993), *Training Skills and Company Competitiveness: A Comparison of Matched Plants in Northern Ireland and Germany*, NIERC Report, Northern Ireland Economic Research Centre, Belfast.

Rostas, L. (1948), *Industrial Production, Productivity and Comparative Productivity in British and American Industry*, Cambridge University Press, Cambridge.

Rowthorn, R. and Wayne, N. (1988), *Northern Ireland: The Political Economy of Conflict*, Pluto Press, London.

RSA (1998a), 'The Minimum Wage', *Regions: The Newsletter of the Regional Studies Association*, no. 213, Regional Studies Association, London, p.6.

RSA (1998b), 'Agenda 2000: Implications for the Structural Funds', *Regions: The Newsletter of the Regional Studies Association*, no. 213, Regional Studies Association, London, p.22-7.

Scottish Office (1993), 'Statistical Bulletin', *Industry Series*, no. IND/1993/A3.5, Government Statistical Service, Edinburgh.

Scott, R. and O'Reilly, M. (1992), *Northern Ireland Export Survey 1990*, NIERC Report, Northern Ireland Economic Research Centre, Belfast.

Sectoral Development Committee (1985), *Report and Recommendations on the Technological Capacity of Indigenous Irish Industry*, Report, no. 8, Government Publications Sales Office, Dublin.

Sheehan, M. and Tomlinson, M. (1996), 'Long-term Unemployment in Belfast', in E. McLaughlin and P. Quirk (eds), *Policy Aspects of Employment Equality in Northern Ireland*, Standing Advisory Commission on Human Rights, Belfast.

Simpson, J. (1993), *Nearly a Single Market But Not Quite*, Business (Belfast) Telegraph, 8 June.

Smith, A.D., Hitchens, D.M.W.N. and Davies, S.W (1982), *International Industrial Productivity: A Comparison of Britain, America and Germany*, Cambridge University Press, Cambridge.

SOEC (1988a), *Price Structure of the Community Countries in 1985*, Statistical Office of the European Communities, Office for Official Publications of the European Communities, Luxembourg.

SOEC (1988b), *Purchasing Power Parities and Gross Domestic Product in Real Terms Results 1985*, Statistical Office of the European Communities, Office for Official Publications of the European Communities, Luxembourg.

SOEC (1989a), *National Accounts ESA Detailed Tables by Branch 1989*, Statistical Office of the European Communities, Office for Official Publications of the European Communities, Luxembourg.

SOEC (1989b), *Gas Prices 1980-1988*, Statistical Office of the European Communities, Office for Official Publications of the European Communities, Luxembourg.

SOEC (1990), *Structure and Activity of Industry 1986-87*, Statistical Office of the European Communities, Office for Official Publications of the European Communities, Luxembourg.

SOEC (1994), *National Accounts ESA Detailed Tables by Branch 1987-1992*, Statistical Office of the European Communities, Office for Official Publications of the European Communities, Luxembourg.

SOEC (1995), *Comparison in Real Terms of the Aggregates of ESA Results for 1992 and 1993*, Statistical Office of the European Communities, Office for Official Publications of the European Communities, Luxembourg.

SOEC (1996), *Statistics in Focus, Economy and Finance, Corrigendum*, no. 5, Statistical Office of the European Communities, Office for Official Publications of the European Communities, Luxembourg.

Soskice, D.W. (1993), 'Social Skills from Mass Higher Education: Rethinking the Company-Based Initial Training Paradigm', *Oxford Review of Economic Policy*, vol. 9, no. 3, pp. 101-13.

Stanners, D. and Bourdeau, P. (1995), *Europe's Environment The Dobris Assessment*, European Environmental Agency, Copenhagen.

Spencer, J.E. and Whittaker, J. (1986), *The Northern Ireland Agriculture Industry: Its Past Development and Medium Term Prospects*, Report to the Economic and Social Research Council, Queen's University Belfast.

Stabler, J.C. and Howe, E.C. (1988), 'Service Exports and Regional Growth in the Post-industrial Era', *Journal of Regional Science*, no. 28, pp. 303-16.

Steedman, H. and Wagner, K. (1987), 'A Second Look at Productivity, Machinery and Skills in Britain and Germany', *National Institute Economic Review*, no. 122, pp. 84-95.

Steedman, H. and Wagner, K. (1989), 'Productivity, Machinery and Skills: Clothing Manufacturing in Britain and Germany', *National Institute Economic Review*, no. 128, pp. 40-57.

TEA (1991), *Strategy*, Training and Employment Agency, Belfast.

TEA (1996), *The Northern Ireland Labour Market: An Overview*, Training and Employment Agency, Belfast.

Teague, P., 'Discrimination and Fair Employment in Northern Ireland', in P. Teague (ed.), *The Northern Ireland Economy*, Lawrence and Wishart, London, pp. 141-69.

Telesis (Report), (1982), *Review of Industrial Policy*, National Economic and Social Council, Report no. 64, Dublin.

Times (The) (1993), *A Bomb for All Bigots*, 27 October.

Times(The) (1998), *Beef Hopes Rise as Europe Lets in Ulster Exports*, 5 March.

Times (The) (1998), *Ulster's Bloody Toll*, 14 May.

Tomlinson, M. (1995), 'Can Britain Leave Ireland? The Political Economy of Peace and War', *Race and Class*, vol. 37, no. 1.

Trimble, D. (1998), 'Ulster Should Say Yes', *Daily Telegraph*, 13 April.

Wagner, K. and van Ark, B. (1996), *International Productivity Differences: Measurement and Explanation*, North Holland, Amsterdam.

Walsh, B. (1997), *Explaining the Republic of Ireland's Economic Transformation*, paper presented to The Two Economies - North and South Conference, Stormont Hotel, Belfast, 28 February.

Weber, M. (1930), *The Protestant Ethic and the Spirit of Capitalism*, Allen and Unwin, London.

WEF (1991), *The World Competitiveness Report*, World Economic Forum, Geneva.

Wilson, T. (1955), *Ulster under Home Rule*, Oxford University Press, Oxford.

Wilson, T. (1989), *Ulster: Conflict and Consent*, Blackwell, Oxford.

Yuill, D., Allen, K., Bachtler, J., Clement, K. and Wishlade, F. (1995), *European Regional Incentives 1995-96*, fifteenth edition, European Policies Research Centre, University of Strathclyde, Bower Saur, London.

Winters, L.A. and Wang, Z.K. (1994), *Eastern Europe's International Trade*, Manchester University Press, Manchester.

For Product Safety Concerns and Information please contact our EU representative GPSR@taylorandfrancis.com Taylor & Francis Verlag GmbH, Kaufingerstraße 24, 80331 München, Germany

Batch number: 10782397

Printed by Printforce, the Netherlands